WALK TALL

Affirmations for People of Color

WALK TALL

Affirmations for People of Color

CARLEEN BRICE

BEACON PRESS

Boston

Beacon Press
25 Beacon Street
Boston, Massachusetts 02108-2892

Beacon Press books
are published under the auspices of
the Unitarian Universalist Association of Congregations.

Printed in the United States of America

03 02 01 8 7 6 5 4 3 2

First published as a paperback by RPI Publishing, Inc. in 1994.

Text Permissions follow the index.
Some African text art from *African Designs from Traditional Sources* by Geoffrey Williams. Copyright © 1971 by Dover Publications, Inc. Used by permission.

Cover art from *Signs and Symbols: African Images in African-American Quilts* by Maude Southwell Wahlman. Copyright © 1993.

Library of Congress Catalog Card Number: 97-73801

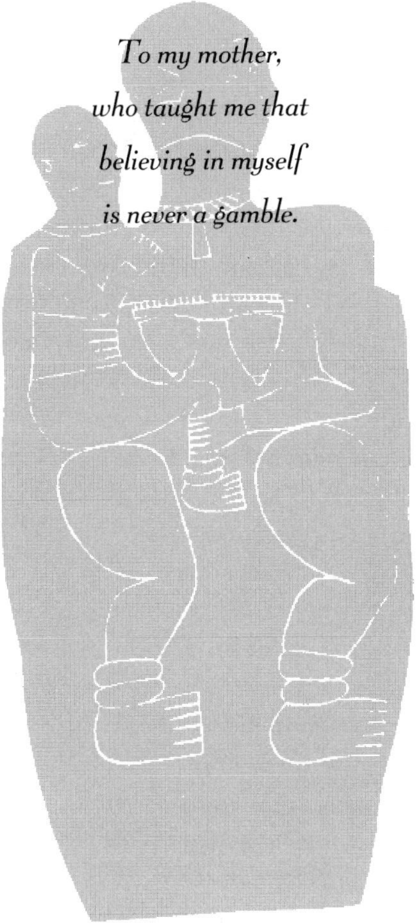

To my mother,
who taught me that
believing in myself
is never a gamble.

Acknowledgments

I have deep feelings of gratitude and love for all of the following people who gave me the strength to express my thoughts and feelings. Many thanks to:

Marie Stilkind for referring me to RPI; Bob Manley and Valerie Deilgat for believing in my manuscript, and Judy, Michele, and Jerry at RPI for their assistance; Jan Johnson for her insightful and wise editing suggestions; Diane Donaldson for her eagle eyes and forever friendship; Marion Steeples for providing me with a steady supply of chocolate (and encouragement) while I finished this book; all my friends at Colorado State University, including Linda Ahuna, Director, Services for Asian-American Students, Lupe Salazar, Director, El Centro/Hispanic Student Services, and Carolyn Fiscus, Director, Native American Student Services, for their input and support; all my friends in Fort Collins for the many, many times they were there for me; Jana Marzano for encouraging me to accept my "assignment from the universe"; and the knowledgeable and courteous staff of the National Writers' Association, Denver Public Library, and the Hue-Man Experience and Tattered Cover bookstores for answering zillions of questions.

I also want to say how much I love and appreciate my family: the Brices, Meltons, Walls, Halls, Nareds, and Boggesses. And, finally, muchas smooches to Robert, who influenced this book and me in innumerable ways.

Introduction

I'm very tall, especially for a woman. While I never developed the hunched shoulders that many tall girls get in their efforts to fit in with shorter friends, I have had times in my life when I had an internal slouch. Externally, I was "walking tall" but inside my spirit was drooping.

My endeavors to bolster my self-esteem included therapy, participation in a Twelve-Step group, and a great deal of reading. I learned that our childhood experiences affect our perceptions, behaviors, and choices even after we have grown up. If we suffered neglect or abuse as children, we likely will have difficulties as adults. We must discover why and how our problems developed to solve them. This type of exploration demands honesty, courage, and the desire to know the truth. It's painful to acknowledge that the people we trusted when we were young mistreated us. And we probably will feel angry and victimized by what we learn during the therapeutic process. But that acknowledgment is only the beginning. Next we must recognize how we have abused ourselves and others. This step of taking responsibility for who we are and where we are ultimately frees us from empty, self-defeating lifestyles. For when we take responsibility for our problems, we obtain the power to solve them.

Scores of self-help books have been written to help people overcome the scars of childhood trauma that manifest themselves in depression, addictions, and relationship problems. *Walk Tall* is designed to help people of color explore those issues and one more: racism. We need to examine the deep scars racism has left on our psyches if we are to overcome its effects. We must feel the hurt, anger, and grief, and then take that next difficult step, which is to assume responsibility for how we have internalized racist beliefs and unconsciously contributed to our own subjugation.

I'm not suggesting that we are responsible for the oppression we experience. Nor am I saying that we have control over racist people. Just as we can't erase what happened to us as children, we can't make racism disappear. However, through self-love and self-respect we *can* stop buying into negative stereotypes and stop acting like victims. We *can* own our power as strong, vital, and creative people. We *can* reclaim our sacred selves.

The sacred self is the inner self that is whole, pure, and in tune with God; it is the spiritual guide that leads us on our paths. We are all born with a sacred self but fear, rage, and resentment can bury it and cause us to lose our way.

Reading this book won't take the place of involvement in spiritual practice, support groups, or personal therapy if that's where your path leads. Rather, I hope these daily messages provide you additional sustenance on your journey toward truth. Each reading ends with an affirmation to help you believe in yourself and your abilities. Read and write the affirmations to help change negative thoughts into positive beliefs and effective actions.

Allow the quotes from people of color who have already walked the path or who are fellow travelers to nourish you. Let their strength, wisdom, and courage counsel and uplift you. Take heart that you are not alone. Best wishes to you on your quest! Walk tall.

—cyb

Renewal *January 1*

Take a day to heal from the lies you've told yourself and that have been told to you. — MAYA ANGELOU

TODAY IS A DAY FOR BEGINNINGS, fresh starts, and New Year's resolutions. Let it also be a day for renewal and healing. Let's cleanse our minds and hearts of fears, hurts, and resentments. The past is behind us; let's learn from it and then release it.

Use this day to reflect on choices and their consequences. Use this day to forgive ourselves and to release others from long-held grudges. Use this day to restore our hope and optimism so that we may create a better world for our children.

Use this day to ask pointed questions of ourselves. Are we using our time wisely, being true to ourselves and our purpose? Are we living honestly and humbly? Are we loving one another as we should?

Use this day to commune with spirit. Pray for joy, serenity, peace, courage, guidance, and willingness. Pray for blessings for everyone we know, including those who have hurt us. Today, let's practice the three Rs: reflect, release, and renew.

I begin this new year with a loving heart and an open mind.

MANY OF US WERE TAUGHT TO THINK of ourselves only after everyone else in the family was taken care of. We were taught that doing for others first was how to show love. Putting ourselves first was considered selfish. But we cannot truly give to another until we give to ourselves.

If we have neglected ourselves, we must focus on what we want or need and give it to ourselves. We could make a list of all that would make us happy—a vacation, a nap, a warm bath, a new outfit, cookies and milk—and choose at least one pleasant activity to do today. Of course, a new car might not be feasible, but maybe a long drive in the country in your present car will do for now.

It's OK to take care of ourselves. It's not only OK, it's wise to be good to ourselves. When we treat ourselves well, we don't expect others to take care of us. When we treat ourselves well, we are more confident, positive, and self-assured. To love ourselves is to teach ourselves that we deserve kindness, gentleness, happiness, and joy.

I take care of myself by doing one thing that I enjoy today.

Freedom *January 3*

GENERATIONS OF PEOPLE HAVE fought for us to be free from slavery, oppression, prejudice. Native American chiefs, African-American preachers, Mexican-American labor leaders, and Asian-American politicians are among those who led the charge for our emancipation. These leaders fought for us to be able to vote and to live, to work, and to go to school wherever we choose.

Political and social freedoms are important. But these freedoms are just the beginning. We must discover our identity to really be free. We must listen to our inner voices, cultivate our characters, and treasure our uniqueness. Freedom means honoring what we know deep in our hearts to be right for us...no matter what society says, no matter what our families, friends, co-workers, or neighbors think.

It's not easy. People might not like us if we disagree with them; they might not like us if we choose differently from them. But we must be true to ourselves in order to be genuinely free.

I discover who I am by looking within. That is real freedom.

∵ ∵ ∵ ∵ ∵ ∵ ∵ ∵ ∵ ∵ ∵ ∵ ∵ ∵ ∵ ∵ ∵

Focus on the Positive *January 4*

IT MAY BE HARD FOR US TO THINK POSItively. Looking at the history of people of color in America, we may think that it is wiser not to get our hopes up. We remember the struggles of our grandparents and parents and think, "It's no use." We look at the injustices we see today and grow depressed. Pretty soon, we just plod along trying to get by, hoping for a better day but not really expecting things to improve.

Expecting good to come to us is a risk. But it's a risk we long to take. As children, we believed. We believed in Santa Claus, the Easter Bunny, our parents,...God. And, as adults, we long for something to believe in—something real. Some of us know we can believe in God. But we may not know we also can believe in ourselves and in our ability to create positive outcomes in our lives.

If it's a better job we want, maybe we need to go back to school. A better relationship may mean we need to learn how to communicate. Whatever it is we want, we can get it...if we believe we can. That's the only way positive change happens. We move forward when we think positively.

I trust myself, God, and the process of life.

The Winter Blues *January 5*

MANY PEOPLE—PARTICULARLY those who live in cold, snowy climates—get depressed during winter. The dreary, oppressive weather limits our activities and affects our mood. Staying indoors causes cabin fever. The lack of sunlight even affects some people's temperament.

But winter doesn't have to be depressing. We can use the days we are inside to reflect about what we want to accomplish in the coming year. We can use the time to read good books to educate and inspire ourselves. We can use the time to get to know our friends and families.

If the winter blues have got us down, we can focus on all the enjoyable aspects of the season: toasty fires in the fireplace, hot chocolate, new-fallen snow, making snow angels, and how funny children look bundled up in their snowsuits. If that doesn't work, we can remind ourselves there are only seventy-three more days until spring!

I let the light within me shine, warming myself and those around me.

We Count *January 6*

But through the process of amendment, interpretation, and court decision, I have finally been included in "We, the people."

—BARBARA JORDAN

SOMETIMES WE BELIEVE THAT OUR FEELings, thoughts, opinions, wants, and needs are secondary. And we act out that belief by not speaking up for ourselves, avoiding confrontation with others. We tell ourselves it's easier to keep quiet. . . . But it's not. Every time we remain silent, we covertly reinforce that old belief that we don't matter. . . . But we do.

We count. What we think, feel, like, and dislike are important. And we don't have to pretend otherwise.

I have the right to think and feel however I choose, and I let my opinions be known.

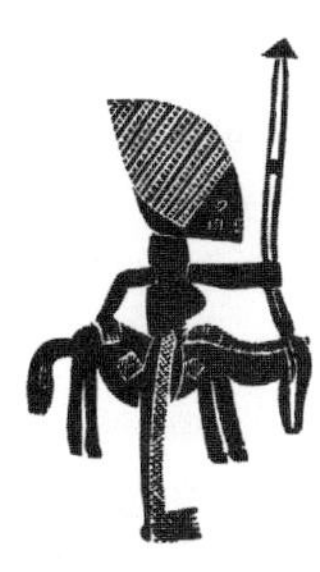

WE DON'T HAVE TO WAIT FOR SOMEone else to be the leader. If we see something in our neighborhood or community that needs improvement, we can take the initiative. We can write a petition; create a neighborhood association; or start a parents' group at our children's school.

Sometimes the first step to becoming a leader is to be a joiner. Are there worthy organizations or activities that already exist that need our support? We don't have to give lots of money. Frequently, groups need volunteers more than funds.

Too often we look to the established leaders to direct events. It's time each one of us realized our own leadership potential. Let's begin today.

I am a leader and take action on what I want to improve.

Art of Living *January 8*

HERE'S A SHORT EXERCISE: CLOSE your eyes and picture your life as a work of art—a novel, song, sculpture, or painting. What are the words, sounds, shapes, textures, and colors you see?

Now, open your eyes. Is this what you want your life to say, sound like, or look like? If not, you can change it. We create our lives every second of the day through our decisions. Perhaps we have gotten into a rut and need to add spice to our lives. We can try something new like taking a different route to work, skipping the cheeseburger and trying a vegetarian lunch, watching a foreign film, learning how to swim, or discovering other activities we would find enjoyable and challenging. The purpose is to pay attention to the everyday choices we make.

I am a great artist and my life is a fresh canvas on which I create works of beauty.

Boundaries, Not Barriers *January 9*

MANY OF US WHO HAVE BEEN HURT or deceived try to protect ourselves by keeping others at a distance. We think we will be safer if we don't let people get to know us. We think people can't hurt us if we do not trust them. We close ourselves up and never tell what is in our hearts and minds. We think we are creating boundaries, but really we are creating barriers.

Boundaries are healthy standards and rules we develop for ourselves that teach others how to treat us. For example, we can have boundaries that say we don't like to be called late at night, we don't want to be teased about our weight, or that we want others to tell us the truth. Boundaries can protect us from abuse. Boundaries allow healthy trust to develop.

We want boundaries, not barriers.

I knock down my walls and build boundaries.

Being Truthful *January 10*

IT CAN BE DIFFICULT TO TELL A LOVED one something we believe will hurt their feelings, even if it's the truth. But if we speak honestly with only concern for their welfare at heart, then we are doing them a favor. We can be compassionate about how and when we deliver the information, but we should not delay the conversation out of fear of offending them. Confronting friends who drink, overeat, work too much, or otherwise abuse or neglect themselves is an act of love.

Confrontation is an act of love that applies to ourselves as well. Perhaps we are the ones who have been challenged by caring people to face the truth. It's not easy hearing negative comments about ourselves, but it can be helpful if a friend shares observations about behavior of which we aren't aware.

As the saying goes, "The truth will set you free, but first it will make you pretty uncomfortable."

I am willing to speak and hear the truth about myself and others.

Good Enough — *January 11*

Let me show you my wounds: my stumbling mind, my "excuse me" tongue, and this nagging preoccupation with the feeling of not being good enough. — LORNA DEE CERVANTES

HAVE YOU EVER BEEN AROUND SOMEone who tries to impress you by bragging about how much they own or how much they make? Do you know a perfectionist—someone who can't sleep with dirty dishes in the sink or leave the office until every paper is off the desk? Or perhaps you know someone who is constantly criticizing himself and others?

These are signs of people who suffer from that nagging feeling of not being good enough. If we feel bad about ourselves, our decisions are not going to be ones that move us forward. The way to make beneficial changes in our lives is to act from a positive frame of mind—not to obsess about perfection. In Twelve-Step programs they say, "Progress not perfection."

If you believe in spiritual law, then you know there is a reason and purpose for everything and everyone. You are good enough exactly as you are. God put you here...what more evidence do you need?

There is no need to blame or shame myself. I am good enough.

Bitterness *January 12*

MANY OF US HOLD ON TO ANGER ABOUT racism until it becomes bitterness. We think bitterness keeps us fueled for political and social battles, but resentment eats us up inside and does us more harm than the racists. If we stay bitter, we will react rather than act.

We become more effective activists when we feel and release our emotions. This doesn't mean that anger about oppression isn't justified. It means that if we are to do something about that which makes us angry, we need to be focused and clearheaded. We need to think before we act.

Get in touch with your anger. Learn the lesson it is trying to teach you. Then act on it and let it go.

I express my anger in a meaningful way and then release it.

FAR TOO MANY PEOPLE OF COLOR GET negative messages about our physical characteristics. We are told directly and indirectly our skin is too light or too dark. Our hair is too nappy or too straight. Our noses too big. Our lips too thick. Our eyes too slanted…

These are lies! Our skin cannot be *too* anything. There is no such thing as the perfect hair, eyes, nose, lips. Some of us are roses. Some of us are tulips. There's no need to compare. We are all beautiful because we are God's children. That's the truth.

I am beautiful inside and outside, and my natural radiance shines forth.

Friendship *January 14*

USUALLY WE BECOME CLOSE TO PEOPLE with whom we share common interests, values, and principles and on that foundation build relationships. However, it's rare that two people remain the same throughout the course of any relationship. When we change, it affects the dynamics within our friendships, and the other people could feel threatened. They may even try to stop us from changing.

Their put-downs can be subtle: They might say that working and going to school full-time would be too stressful. Or they tell us we don't need to exercise because we look fine just as we are. Or they advise us to stay in a dead-end job because it provides good benefits... disguising their fear as loving concern.

It is true that a good friend will love and accept us no matter what our educational, financial, or physical condition. But a real friend also will support our efforts to develop to our fullest potential and may even give us a kick in the pants from time to time. A real friend acts as a partner in our growth process by teaching us or allowing us to learn for ourselves. If we are true friends, we clear a path in our relationships for our friends to spread their wings and take flight.

I am an ally to my friends and to myself.

Martin Luther King Jr.'s Birthday *January 15*

THERE'S AN OLD ADAGE THAT GOES "IF you don't stand for something, you'll fall for anything." We have to stand for something in this life. If we think we can avoid responsibility by choosing not to take a stand, we are wrong. If we're not part of the solution, we're part of the problem.

There are many things we can commit to—our personal growth and recovery; the well-being of our children; the welfare of our communities; equal treatment for all people. Whatever it is we believe in, we need to be committed to it and be willing to face the hardships we might encounter along the way.

I honor Dr. King's memory by taking a stand for something I believe in.

Fear of Rejection *January 16*

BEING REJECTED IS ONE OF THE GREATest fears people have. Being ostracized, isolated, or unloved are frightening to us because we need others to survive.

However, we shouldn't allow our fear of rejection to drive us into unhealthy or dishonest situations. When we are afraid of being rejected, we may try to hide our true selves and become what we think others want us to be. Well-adjusted people don't want us to pretend to be someone we're not. They are attracted to what is genuine within us.

What's the antidote for this fear that depletes self-esteem and poisons relationships? The cure for fear of rejection is to love and be true to ourselves, to stop repressing our emotions and opinions in order to be accepted.

We can't lose when we are being true to ourselves. If honesty and sincerity cause us to lose some friends, so be it. We will have the satisfaction of personal integrity and the knowledge that the people who are with us love us for who we really are. That's worth more than all the fair-weather friends in the world!

Being rejected by others isn't the worst that can happen to us. It would be far worse to reject ourselves.

I am not afraid of rejection. I know the rewards that come with being true to myself.

COURAGE IS NOT AN ABSENCE OF fear. Courage is working to achieve our goals in spite of fear. As long as we are growing and learning, we will continually be faced with challenges. Each new situation will bring opportunity and probably a little fear. Will we succeed? Will we be able to cope? What will happen to us if we fail?

What we think about, we give power to. So let's stop concentrating on fearful thoughts and give energy to motivating ideas. We can remind ourselves how we mastered a similarly difficult situation. We can remember a time when we thought all was lost, yet we survived. We can encourage ourselves with affirmations and turn to others for support.

We also can focus on the opportunities for learning in every situation. If we are aware and willing, we can learn even from failure or tragedy. No matter what we are afraid of, we can handle it. We are never alone. The spirits of our ancestors always walk with us. With courage, we can face our fears.

Though I may be afraid, I face life head on today. I know I can cope with whatever life dishes out.

La Raza *January 18*

We shall all be alike—brothers of one father and one mother, with one sky above us and one country around us, and one government for all. —CHIEF JOSEPH

LA *RAZA,* "THE RACE," IS USED TO describe the feeling of togetherness and kinship that bond people of Mexican descent. All of us—Hispanic, African-American, Asian-American, Native American, and Anglos—belong to the only race there is: the human race. We share a common lineage and ultimately the same family.

No matter how your Higher Power manifests itself to you—Jesus, Buddha, Oladumare, Grandmother/Great Spirit, Mohammed—it is the same force within us all. The same blood runs through my veins as yours. I feel the same longing for acceptance and belonging echo in my heartbeat as you do. The same fire of ambition burns in my belly that burns in yours. We are much more alike than we are different.

Today, let's focus on the traits we share and encourage bonds of kinship that stretch across race, religion, and ethnicity.

I am connected to others by a union of heart and mind.

Participation *January 19*

LIFE IS NOT A SPECTATOR SPORT. How many of us just watch the events in our lives without really participating? Let's not be voyeurs of our own lives. Let's fully, actively participate.

Participating in our lives means accepting challenges rather than hiding from opportunities. We try to solve our problems rather than running away from them. We take risks rather than seeking the security of bad habits and boring behavior.

Life is meant to be savored. Let's relish all the moments we are given. Today, let's get in the game.

I step off the sidelines and join in the game of life.

FOR MOST OF US, A HYPHEN IS MUCH more than a punctuation mark. The hyphen that connects our dual heritage also means making choices about how to reconcile our two selves, our American part and our Thai, Brazilian, African, Indian, Mexican, Chinese, Japanese, Colombian, or Korean part.

Some of us shed our ethnic ways and try to assimilate into the dominant culture immediately. We might willingly give up our language, ceremonies, and traditions and accept the ways of the majority. Others attempt to live in the United States ignoring everything about American culture. We might hold on to our countries' ways for dear life.

There is a third choice. We don't have to choose between our ethnic ancestry and our American heritage. We can choose what we like from both cultures. We can speak Chinese and English. We can eat beans and rice and hamburgers and hot dogs. We can listen to Julio Iglesias and Janet Jackson. We can wear kente cloths and business suits.

I don't have to live between two worlds; I can live in both in harmony.

SOMETIMES WE FIND OURSELVES in situations where we feel misunderstood and find it difficult to express ourselves.

One technique we can use to communicate better is using "I" statements. For example, instead of saying "You made me mad," we would say "I feel angry with you because. . . ." By using "I" statements, we speak for ourselves and take responsibility for what we express. We don't claim to know what others are thinking or feeling, and we don't blame them for the way we feel or think.

"I" statements are empowering. Taking responsibility for how we perceive situations opens up the conversation for the other person to respond. Perhaps the person's intention was completely different than what we inferred. Using an "I" statement allows the other person to set the record straight without feeling defensive or attacked.

Communication brings consonance into our lives by acknowledging our own and others' needs to be known and understood. We can make our point by using "I" statements, listening, telling the truth, and demonstrating a willingness to share.

I take responsibility for my thoughts and feelings in my communication with others.

Chinese New Year *January 22*

There is neither being nor non-being but becoming.

—BUDDHA

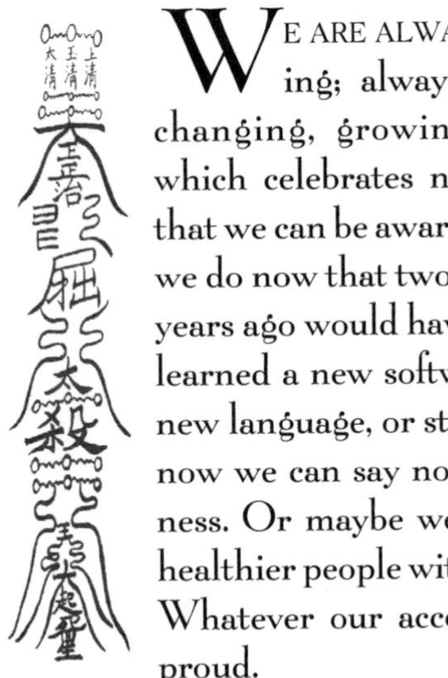

WE ARE ALWAYS IN A STATE OF BECOMING; always in a state of learning, changing, growing. Chinese New Year, which celebrates new beginnings, is a time that we can be aware of our growth. What can we do now that two months, two years, or ten years ago would have been difficult? Have we learned a new software program, mastered a new language, or stopped drinking? Perhaps, now we can say no to people with assertiveness. Or maybe we have learned to identify healthier people with whom to share our lives. Whatever our accomplishments, we can be proud.

We still have goals to achieve. In this new year, we have a fresh start. We don't have to be tied to what was. We can become whatever we chose.

I celebrate "my becoming." I look to the rest of the year with hope and marvel at the possibilities.

A SENSE OF COMMUNITY IS ONE OF OUR strong points that will benefit our country as we move into the next century. This spiritual bond that compels us to care about others can help us heal the wounds of our people. Alcoholism, drug addiction, dysfunctional families, and homelessness are all problems that can be ameliorated with loving attention. With the rise in support groups and volunteerism, the dominant society is beginning to mirror what many of us have known all along: We need each other.

If this country is going to survive, indeed if humankind is going to survive, then the dog-eat-dog days must end. To help solve the world's problems, we must recognize that our family includes all people.

I extend love and support to my community.

Pride *January 24*

THEY SAY THAT PRIDE COMES BEFORE a fall, meaning that arrogance leads to failure. However, pride of self leads to success.

Pride doesn't have to run counter to humility. We can be proud of ourselves and still be modest. We can be proud of accomplishments and still thank God for blessing us, still acknowledge the help we received from friends, family, or colleagues.

When we are proud of ourselves for something we've done, we are actually acknowledging our higher selves; for it is the divine in us that creates good. We are simply being respectful of ourselves. Self-respect and self-praise help raise our self-worth. People with high self-esteem have a deep understanding and healthy regard for how the Creator works in their lives.

Today, we can recognize our accomplishments. If we stood up to a bully, helped an older person carry groceries, landed an account for our company, got an A on a test, or spent the evening reading to a child, we can be proud of ourselves. We've earned our own self-respect and there is no shame in giving it.

I am proud of my wonderful accomplishments.

Promises *January 25*

WHETHER A LEGAL CONTRACT, wedding vow, social commitment, or "pinky swear," a promise is sacred. When we make a promise to someone, we create an expectation that we will meet an obligation. If we break a promise, we fail others and ourselves. Therefore, let's be careful what we promise.

To avoid letting people down, let's be honest. If we know in our hearts we don't want to do a favor, attend a party, or do whatever is being asked of us, we don't have to agree. We can refuse to do the service or decline the invitation. It is better to honestly refuse someone, than to lie to them later.

When we make promises haphazardly, we may become resentful and break our pledge. Breaking promises teaches people to distrust us. Breaking promises also causes us to feel ashamed of ourselves. When we keep our word, we gain self-respect; it feels good to keep a commitment.

If we say we are going to do something, we should do it. Our word is gold; let's not squander it on plans we don't intend to keep. A promise kept is a reputation made.

I keep my promises to myself and others.

Follow-Through *January 26*

Hard work equals success. —OSWALDO ESTRADA

SOMETIMES WE ARE INSPIRED ABOUT something and come up with an idea for a new product, an exciting venture, or an innovative solution to a problem. For a while, we are enthusiastic about our idea, then our eagerness dies.

Getting good ideas is the easy part. The hard part, the part most people don't do, is follow-through. That's the difference between achievers and nonachievers.

Those little bits of creation that pop in our minds happen for a reason. We are meant to accomplish things. If we don't follow through, we'll never know what we can do. Today, let's take action on one project. If you have a good idea for a program at school, tell your professor. If you have a recommendation to correct a problem at work, submit a proposal to your supervisor. If you have a good idea for a career change, find out how to get started.

Today, let's follow our ideas to the destination of success.

I heed the call of my ideas and follow through.

Be Polite *January 27*

TOO OFTEN, WE THINK WE ONLY HAVE to be polite to people we don't know well or to authority figures. Pardon me, but I disagree. It's just as important to be courteous to our friends and family.

Politeness is more than being sociable or tactful. It's more than having people think we are nice people. Politeness is about showing respect and care. Courtesy is about not discounting others. We all want to know that we are appreciated, and we all deserve kindness.

Today, let's be polite. We don't have to behave like those cartoon chipmunks who can't complete a sentence without thanking one another or excusing themselves. But it won't hurt to treat people with deference.

Our elders taught us the importance of having good manners. We learned not to interrupt people when they were speaking, to say hello to people, and to be gracious to guests. While we don't have to be formal with our loved ones, politeness demonstrates that we think they are worthy of our concern. Three of the most important phrases we can say to people are "please," "thank you," and "I'm sorry."

I treat everyone, including myself, with consideration and courtesy

Payoffs *January 28*

WHETHER POSITIVE OR NEGATIVE, there is always a payoff to everything we do. We always receive something back for our efforts; it's the motivation for why we do what we do. Children will try to gain a parent's attention by misbehaving if they feel they can't get their parent's attention through positive means. So if a parent doesn't notice good grades or touchdowns, a child will cut classes or get in fights.

Adults also seek whatever attention is available. We are just as likely to act out if our mates or friends don't notice positive behavior. Negative attention is better than no attention. That is our payoff.

We also get payoffs when we act the martyr. "Poor pitiful me" may get us sympathy and release us from responsibility but at the expense of our self-respect. We get payoffs for staying in bad relationships. We might think that "at least we're not alone." These types of rewards aren't in our best interest.

Today, let's ask ourselves what benefit we receive from our choices. Let's strive for genuine gains, rather than those that encourage negative behavior. Let's reward ourselves for accountable, respectable behavior.

I seek positive payoffs.

Practice Makes Progress *January 29*

IT IS AWESOME TO WATCH SOMEONE AT the peak of their craft. An accomplished actor can make us forget we are watching a movie. A skilled athlete can dazzle us with her grace, strength, and agility. People who are expert at what they do have done two things: discovered their talents and practiced. We must do the same.

It may take a while to discover our natural talents. Discovering our abilities can be fun. We can try many things to find out what we are good at and what we enjoy. We can experiment and explore different fields.

Once we realize our talents, we must practice to master them. Bodybuilders exercise two or three times a day before a competition. Marathon runners run hundreds of miles to prepare for a long-distance race. Musicians play their instruments for hours every day to get ready for a performance.

Be patient. Be gentle. Whether we want to be writers, artists, CEOs, or better mates or parents, the more we practice, the better we get.

I begin to unearth my abilities, knowing that with practice, I can become great.

THERE IS A DIFFERENCE BETWEEN shame and guilt. Guilt is the feeling that lets us know we have violated our principles and morals; we have *done* wrong. Shame is a prevailing belief that no matter what we do we *are* wrong.

People who have been brutalized start to believe that they caused the mistreatment, yet they also know they've done nothing wrong. These thoughts are confusing and cause shame. Children who have been sexually, physically, verbally, or emotionally abused feel shame. So do we who have been enslaved, robbed, raped, forcibly moved, and denied citizenship and human rights.

Shame is most devastating because once we believe we have no value, we shame ourselves over and over. We tell ourselves again and again that we are bad, stupid, ugly, lazy, and worthless. We only know to treat ourselves how we have been treated.

How do we combat shame? Visit a psychologist, participate in a support group, read books about what happened to us, write in a journal. We treat ourselves with compassion. We replace the cruel tapes we replay in our mind with loving messages.

I heal my shame by reminding myself that I may make mistakes, but I am not a mistake.

The Idealized Self — *January 31*

PEOPLE WHO ARE TAUGHT THAT THEY are inferior sometimes pretend to be perfect to cover their feelings of inadequacy. If people have been denied the right to be themselves, they may create an idealized self that they imagine will be more acceptable to others. Nobody can keep up the charade forever and eventually their human frailties come through. They damn themselves for not living up to their grandiose standards. This leads to self-hatred and neurotic pursuits of perfection.

When we shamefully try to hide our shortcomings, we deny ourselves the right to be human. We lead empty lives filled with lies and self-loathing. If all our energy goes toward denying imperfections, how can we really work on ourselves?

We must learn to love and appreciate ourselves with all our "bad points." We can acknowledge our weaknesses without justification or rationalization. Real people with real lives have problems and make mistakes. They also flourish, prosper, love and experience sorrow, as well as joy. "Idealized" people never fully experience either.

I let go of pretentious conceptions about what I think I should be and accept myself as I am—a fallible, wonderful human being.

How in the midst of such death and suffering could we find so much strength to love, so much determination to live, fight on, and be free? In permanent and grueling exile, how could a people dance and create songs and art, fashion institutions of hope, bear so many children of beauty?

—VINCENT HARDING

THIS MONTH WE CELEBRATE THE hopes, dreams, and achievements of African-Americans—people who not only survived persecution, slavery, lynching, discrimination, and subjugation, but triumphed in the midst of it.

This commemoration isn't just for African-Americans. All who have suffered at the hands of racism should celebrate. We've all survived and we can all triumph. During February let's take time to recognize the accomplishments of our people, be they African-American, Hispanic-American, Native American, or Asian-American. Let's be proud of ourselves and lift each other up. It's a spiritual truth that when one of us succeeds, we all succeed.

I celebrate the drive, determination, and spirit that allowed the oppressed people of this country to survive. I, too, will prevail.

"I'VE ALWAYS HATED TO EXERCISE AND I always will." "I know I should be taking classes after work, but I just never get around to it." "I'll write my résumé next week." Sound familiar?

No doubt about it—it's hard to break habits. But we *can* break negative habits by giving up excuses and taking responsibility for our actions. There's much more potency in saying "I choose to quit smoking" than there is in saying "If I get lung cancer, I guess it's just my time to go." Accepting responsibility is only the beginning.

We will need to find assistance with addictions to alcohol, drugs, nicotine, food, or sex. We can't recover alone. There are support groups, therapists, and programs for just about every type of compulsive behavior. Our first step toward breaking a negative habit can be to open the phone book and seek help.

We can break less dangerous habits by substituting a new, healthier habit in place of the old. If we always watch TV in the evening, we can start a new habit of going for a walk right after work or turning on the stereo or reading a book. If we never have enough time to complete our work, we can make a new habit of arriving at the office ten minutes early. Whatever the negative habit, substitute a positive one in its place.

I eliminate bad habits instead of excusing them.

Labels *February 3*

"OVERACHIEVER," "PRETTY," "LONER," "Teacher's Pet," "Youngest Child," "Head of the Family," "Brain," and other labels tell us how we are supposed to be. Because we know what is expected of us, we hide behind our labels. It's safe there, or so we think.

However, if we stay in the shadow of our labels for too long, we may forget they are just names, not who we are. You may know people like this. Adults who still think of themselves as "the baby of the family." Men who try to "boss" their wives and children like their employees. Women who "mother" their co-workers and friends.

We also use labels to put people in categories so we know how to relate to them: She's a bigot or a Christian or a pro-choicer. He's a sexist or an intellectual or a right-winger. The problem is that we can't fully interact with a label. We can only communicate with a human being, faults, talents, hopes and dreams, warts and all.

Labels are just descriptions of parts of our personality. We are so much more!

I take my label off and communicate as a complete person, allowing others to do the same.

Education — *February 4*

Oh, then, turn your attention to knowledge and improvement; for knowledge is power. —MRS. MARIA W. STEWART

光

WE VALUE A GOOD EDUCATION FOR our children. We know that is the way to success and prosperity in this country. However, many of us adults don't realize that our education should be a lifelong progression.

Learning doesn't have to follow a formal process. Life offers lessons every day. All we have to do is be aware of the educational opportunities around us. There are many ways to continue our schooling without going to school. We could probably learn a great deal by helping our children or nieces and nephews with homework. We can visit an art gallery or planetarium. We can learn to make pottery, write poems, or dance ballet.

Or we could enroll in a conventional educational environment. If we've been to college, we can go back and get a Ph.D. or even another bachelor's degree in a different subject. Education is just as valuable for adults as it is for youngsters. Let's take a page out of our children's books and commit ourselves to learning.

I'm alert for opportunities to learn because I know that education is for life.

Right Livelihood *February 5*

IN BUDDHIST PHILOSOPHY, RIGHT LIVE-lihood is one of eight steps to overcome suffering. Buddhists believe that we should make a living through honest means and avoid hurting and debasing others.

We can expand this concept by thinking of right livelihood as accomplishing our mission in life. Each individual has a purpose, something uniquely their own to contribute to the world. We can discover our purpose by looking at what we sincerely enjoy. Do we like reading, teaching, writing, painting, cooking, healing, listening, repairing, building, performing, or helping? Our dreams and wishes are meant to spur us toward reaching our goals. Our talents and strengths are God-given; we are meant to use them for a reason.

Think of all the depression and turmoil associated with doing a job you hate. Being true to your purpose will help you avoid that type of suffering.

I engage in the right livelihood for me.

Sacred Self — *February 6*

The search for an identity is, therefore, usually a search for that lost, pure, true, real, genuine, original, authentic self. . . ."

—TRINH T. MINH-HA

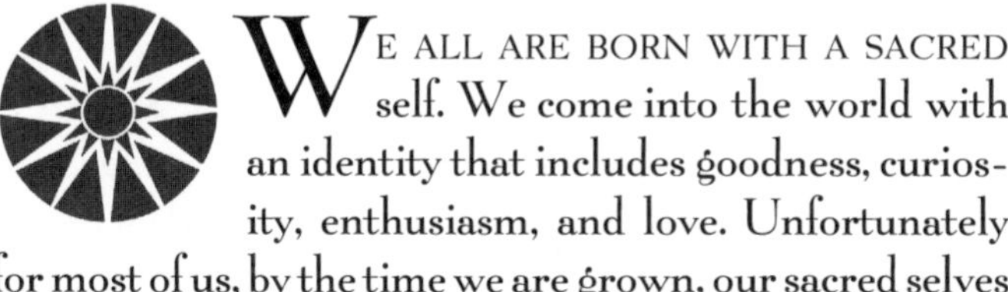

WE ALL ARE BORN WITH A SACRED self. We come into the world with an identity that includes goodness, curiosity, enthusiasm, and love. Unfortunately for most of us, by the time we are grown, our sacred selves are buried under layers of falsehoods and hurts.

But it's never too late to rediscover our authentic self. It's still there. We feel it when we share a laugh with a close friend, hold a baby, read a poem, or tell somebody off. We may have to coax that spontaneous, expansive, honest part of ourselves to come to the surface. But come out it will. Once we decide to be ourselves again, it's only a matter of time!

I reclaim my sacred self.

Explore Your History *February 7*

Know whence you came. If you know whence you came, there is really no limit to where you can go. —James Baldwin

PEOPLE OF COLOR HAVE DUAL histories—as individuals and as members of our races. We can explore our individual history by looking at our childhoods. What values and principles did we adopt from our family, peers, teachers, and society?

It is likely that when we open ourselves to such questions we will note negative as well as positive experiences. It's usually the negative that we bury in our minds to avoid the pain and we need to feel what we have suppressed in order to heal. We may need to forgive those who raised us for not being all we wanted or needed them to be.

We can use a similar process to explore our people's history. Hearing relatives' stories or reading about slavery, reservations, or internment camps may cause us to feel angry or sad. And the emotions are even more intense because we know our people still face injustice and hardship.

It's important to acknowledge the feelings and have them validated by others who understand. But, just as with feelings from childhood, it's also important to release them at an appropriate time.

I feel my repressed emotions for as long as I need to, then when I am ready, I release my anger, fear, and hurt.

Letting Go of the Past *February 8*

EXPLORE YOUR PAST, THEN LET IT go. We are meant to go forward not back. Everything we do adds up to move us further ahead. However, we can't progress if we are stuck in the past. Clinging to happy memories of days gone by is just as destructive as holding on to resentments from the past. We must let go of yesterday to be prepared for tomorrow.

But it's not hard to do, for our ancestors have left us a trail to follow. As Maya Angelou would say, "We have been paid for." Every slave, laborer, immigrant, activist, freedom fighter, preacher, and teacher that has gone before us paid with their ideas, spirit, and blood for us to be here. Let's not let their struggles be in vain. Let's use the advantages gained by the people who came before us. We can reach whatever heights we choose, for we stand on the shoulders of proud, fine people who are more than willing to give us a boost.

I let go of yesterday and focus on today.

"Those" Names   February 9

"THOSE" NAMES. THE SHAMING and maiming names spit at us on playgrounds, whispered behind our backs in offices, and shouted at us from speeding cars.

In "Spic-O-Rama," comedian John Leguizamo takes one of "those" names and turns it against itself. Through humor, Leguizamo owns his power of thought. The word *spic* no longer has the ability to wound.

We too can take back our power. We don't have to let ignorant, insecure people hurt us. *Nigger, Chink, Jap, wetback,* and the rest are just words, but we give them life when we feel ashamed and hurt. We give them life when we believe what they say about us; insults only injure when we think they are true. When we know the truth about who we are, "those" names lose their sting.

We don't have to accept it when someone calls us an insulting name. We should be assertive and tell people what we think of their abusive language. We can do so with dignity and calm without sinking to their level. Insults tell more about the people who use such foul language than they do about us. We do not have to accept abusive treatment from others, nor do we have to let their insults affect our self-esteem.

I know the truth about myself. I am a precious child of God.

Gossip *February 10*

WHEN WE GOSSIP, WE TRY TO boost our self-confidence by favorably comparing ourselves to others. So-and-so cheated on her husband. We think: "I've never done that—I'm a better person than she. I would never do that to my man." Someone got fired for embezzling funds. Our thoughts: "What a thief! I always knew he was no good. I'm good. I don't steal."

Criticizing others is our way of getting those negative voices in our heads to shut up. "See," we tell them, "those people are much worse than me. Can you cut me some slack now?" Only, we don't feel better when we gossip. We feel depressed because deep down inside, we know we are not better than anybody else. So when we ridicule, scorn, or judge others based on their behavior, we mock and reject ourselves.

We improve our self-esteem by noticing and acknowledging the good in other people. We should spend time at the watercooler, barbershop, nightclub, and church praising and appreciating people for their honesty, beauty, integrity, humor, intelligence, and kindness. When we esteem others, we esteem ourselves.

Here's an exercise: Go one full week without criticizing anybody and see what happens. Start today.

Beginning today, I look for the best and find it in everyone I meet.

Wake-up Calls *February 11*

Once you wake up thought in a man, you can never put it to sleep again. —ZORA NEALE HURSTON

SLEEPWALKERS ARE DANGEROUS. THEY bump into walls, or amble restlessly through a dark house until they fall back into bed. In their slumber they can hurt themselves or other people. Some of us act like sleepwalkers even when we are awake, stumbling through life unaware of the relationship between our actions and their consequences. The danger day-sleepwalkers face is they miss opportunities for change and growth.

The old wives' tale says it is harmful to rouse a sleepwalker but awakening is what saves day-sleepwalkers. We may have experienced wake-up calls in the form of illness, divorce, or job loss. When things like this happen, it's natural to feel sad, disappointed, and despairing. However, it is helpful to think of such events as alarm clocks that alert us to important matters in our lives. Once awakened, we can resolve the root issues that cause heartache. When we are cognizant, we can easily avoid problems that would trip us if we were asleep.

Walk through life wide-eyed and aware, watching for opportunities and danger signs.

I'm grateful for whatever alarm clocks sound today. They're my cue to wake up.

WE MAY VIEW OURSELVES PRIMARILY as parents, entrepreneurs, children, siblings, mates, or students. But our idea of who we think we are will shift with time. As we grow, long-held opinions will give way to information gathered from new experiences. We may change political and religious affiliations. Our primary family roles may change from child to spouse to parent. Our professional image may change from rookie to manager to CEO. But our spiritual identity remains the same.

Our spiritual identity is our soul, our spirit, and it never changes. We can build and enhance our characters. We can grow and develop. But who we are at our core never changes. Indeed, the surface changes we experience may help us discover our true identity. We may have to go through several evolutions before we find out who we are and what we have to give.

We are always children of God. We are always good and valuable people. No matter who you think you are, your real identity is a beloved child of the universe. Keep knowledge of who you are close to your heart no matter what role you play in life.

No matter how I change, I know I am always worthwhile.

Balance *February 13*

WE HAVE MANY COMMITMENTS that take our time and energy. Professional and social obligations often conflict with personal responsibilities to family, friends and self. Though our careers and relationships are important, we need to construct a balance between them and the time required for our development.

If our focus is on achieving a goal that demands much concentration, we might have to scale back other areas. The busy executive who is trying to make his or her way up the corporate ladder may not be able to spend much time with family members. The parent might decide to put his or her career on hold until the children are older.

However, even though we want to achieve our goals, we still need balance. We can focus on our top priority and build in time for other aspects of life. Business people can schedule regular activities with family and be emotionally available so that quality time is spent with their family. Stay-at-home parents can do volunteer work and serve the community while devoting most of their time to their children. With creativity, commitment, and willingness, we can develop ways to create balance in our lives and still achieve our goals.

I set priorities and let go of activities that don't help meet my goals or create balance.

Valentine's Day *February 14*

My friends, how desperately do we need to be loved and to love.
—CHIEF DAN GEORGE

TODAY IS A DAY TO DEMONSTRATE OUR love to our spouses, lovers, families, and friends. Chocolates, flowers, and cards are traditionally how we display our affection for others on Valentine's Day.

We can also show our love by listening, and *really hearing what our loved ones have to say.* We can show our love by supporting and encouraging them in their endeavors. We can show our love by honestly communicating our feelings and allowing them to do the same.

We can show people we love them by working at maintaining our relationships. Long-term relationships, especially, can become stale and unsatisfying unless we are willing to work to keep them fresh and interesting. That means we listen when we don't feel like listening. We talk when we don't feel like talking. And we stay together when we don't feel like staying together.

This is not to suggest that we deny our needs and become people pleasers. We acknowledge that healthy relationships call for reciprocity. All parties in the relationship are allowed to give and receive.

I give my love today, which is better than anything that could be purchased in a store.

IT IS ABUSIVE TO TELL CHILDREN THAT they are stupid for painting a purple elephant or reprimand them because they talk to invisible friends. Scolding them for being inventive teaches them to distrust their instincts and to discount their imagination.

When people have been abused, their ability to be creative is often one of the first things they lose. Being creative requires spontaneity and permission to be different, which is difficult for people who have been mistreated. They often feel different from others and want to fit in with people they perceive to be "normal." In their efforts to assimilate, they lose their own unique spark, their own voice.

The good news is that no matter how much our creativity is stifled, when we decide to get it back we can. We can learn to cherish what makes us different. We can encourage unconventional behavior and offbeat thoughts. We can get those creative juices rolling.

Pink alligators, talking dogs, and green clouds are waiting to be discovered. It's time to own our creativity once again.

I let my inner child come out and teach me how to play.

Self-Centeredness *February 16*

SELF-CENTERED PEOPLE ARE IMMATURE. Part of our developmental process is learning that other people weren't put on this planet to serve us. Children learn this when they discover that their mothers and fathers have separate lives from them.

Sometimes we still act as if we are the center of the universe. This works two ways. One, is that we think what is happening in our lives is so important that nobody else matters. We should honor ourselves and treat ourselves with respect and give ourselves time and attention. However, we also need to have empathy for what others are experiencing.

The other part of center-of-the-universe thinking is that we take responsibility for other people and think we are to blame for their every thought and action. The boss sets a new policy for the staff—our fault. Our spouse is late for work—our fault. Our friend ignores us—our fault. Self-centered people have an inflated view of their influence on people.

While the roles we play are important to the scheme of things, we are simply one part of the divine plan. The real center of life is God.

I know my place in the world.

At a Crossroads *February 17*

MANY OF US WILL COME TO A POINT IN our lives where we must choose which path to take. We can learn from experiences on either road, however, one path may be more beneficial than the other. The "right" road is the one that teaches us what we need to learn to fulfill our mission on this earth. No one can tell us which is the right road, we must determine that for ourselves.

We can look for guideposts to help us decide. Are there danger signs along one path and welcome signs on the other? We must look deeper than the surface. Just because one path is covered with trees and vines and will be difficult to follow doesn't mean it isn't right for us.

If we are at a crossroads and don't know which direction to take, we can ask the Great Spirit to show us the way. We can ask the universal light within us to shine on our journey. We can trust that the way will become clear.

The fork in the road is a sacred spot that holds the potential for spiritual illumination. I am grateful when I approach a crossroads.

JAPS...
Their tongues / are yellow / with "r's" / with "l's."
They hate / themselves / on the sly. I / used to be
Japanese.

—LAWSON FUSAO INADA

SOME OF US HAVE BEEN TEASED about the way we talk. Maybe our accents hinder the way we pronounce English words or the grammar we use is incorrect. Denying us our original languages was one tool of oppression. Our mother tongues were not English. Our people spoke Spanish, Navajo, Swahili, Chinese, Lakota, Japanese, and a host of other dialects.

Our people have contributed much to the English language: *Savanna, mahogany, chipmunk,* and *jaguar* are among the five hundred words from Native American languages that Americans use. Mexicans contributed *coyote, chocolate, tomatoes,* and *rodeo.* African slaves contributed words like *bananas, yams,* and *banjo.* We get words like *tea,* and *kumquat* from the Chinese. *Bandanna, dungaree,* and *juggernaut* can be traced to India. *Algebra, alcohol,* and *assassin* are Arabic offerings.

We don't have to be ashamed of how we or our people speak. We can take pride in the way our languages have added to the American experience.

I take pride in my language.

TODAY, LET'S SET ASIDE A FEW MINUTES to pray in whichever form we feel comfortable. We can go to a mosque, temple, church, synagogue, or other holy place. We can be with nature and kneel beside a river, mountain, or tree. We can be in our homes, offices, or cars. We can join with others or be alone.

Let's pray for health, happiness, and healing. Let's pray for society to experience a spiritual awakening so that all will value each other and the earth. Let's pray to open our hearts to love.

We can talk to our Higher Power and share our hopes, fears, dreams, and worries. Or we can say one of the simplest and best prayers: Thank you.

My prayers bring wisdom and serenity.

The Company We Keep — February 20

PEOPLE JUDGE US BY THE COMPANY we keep, but more important we can judge ourselves by the company we keep. Not that we should be snobs about who we make friends with. However, we should make sure that the people we make friends with are sincere, scrupulous, and ethical.

People attract relationships that reflect their mental and emotional states. Therefore, people with high self-worth attract well-adjusted people. People with low self-esteem often find themselves in failed relationship after failed relationship. If our friends and acquaintances are healthy people, it is a sign that we care enough about ourselves to involve ourselves with people who can take care of themselves and meet our needs. If our companions aren't so healthy, we need to ask ourselves why we are involved with them. Do we want to fix them? Do we think we are undeserving of peaceful, supportive relationships? Have we only been concerned with superficial characteristics—like looks or money—and not selected friends based on their values?

Today, let's evaluate our relationships and determine what they say about us. Look into your friend's eyes. Do they mirror the self you want to see?

I measure the company I keep to determine my *maturity.*

Grief Process

February 21

Death will come, always out of season. —BIG ELK

THE DEATH OF A FRIEND OR FAMILY member is traumatic. People who lose someone they love often experience a set of similar thoughts and emotions called "the grief process."

The first stage is shock and denial. Denial is our way of protecting ourselves until we are ready to handle the pain. Some also experience deep sadness and longing for their deceased loved one, accompanied by confusion and disorientation. Others may feel angry at themselves, God, or the person who died. Finally, there is resolution and acceptance of the death.

However, the grief process is not an orderly progression from stage to stage. It's confusing, and uncomfortable. People may think they are finished grieving, only to find themselves crying when they hear the deceased's name once again feeling like they can't accept that the person is gone.

If we are grieving, the best thing we can do is allow ourselves to feel however we feel. It's OK if we want to cry. And it's OK if we can't cry right now. There is no correct way to grieve. More than anything, we will need to be tender and gentle with ourselves.

I treat myself with kindness when I grieve.

Choices *February 22*

EVERY DAY WE MAKE CHOICES. WE are probably more conscious of the simple choices we make, like what to wear and what to eat. But we also make more important decisions about our lives. We decide how we're going to feel. We decide what we're going to think. And we decide how we're going to be.

These are the decisions that dictate our lives. Sometimes we feel overwhelmed by our choices and are afraid of the consequences of making the wrong decision. Deciding not to decide is a choice and it teaches us to distrust ourselves. It may be better to suffer the consequences of a poor choice than to have someone else make the decision for us.

We have freedom of thought and the power to make choices. We are capable of choosing what is in our best interest. We can trust ourselves. Whatever we want to be, do, or have, we can. Today, let's become more conscious of the choices we make.

I am aware of the choices I make every day and honor my God-given power of choice.

Self-Help — *February 23*

Help yourself as you travel along in life. The earth has many narrow passages scattered over it. If you have something with which to strengthen yourself, then when you get to these passages, you will be able to pass them safely and your fellow men will respect you.

—CRASHING THUNDER

PEOPLE IN TWELVE-STEP GROUPS practice *HALT*, which means members stop before they get too hungry, angry, lonely, or tired. Twelve-steppers know they can handle the narrow passages much better if they are physically, mentally, emotionally, and spiritually strong.

We prepare ourselves for the rough roads we may face ahead by fueling our bodies with wholesome meals and plenty of rest; fortifying our minds by reading challenging material and engaging in intellectual discussion; and nourishing our spirits through prayer, meditation, or spending time with people we love.

Rather than waiting until the going gets tough to seek help, we can strengthen ourselves before we get to the narrow passages. This is the meaning of self-help.

I nurture and nourish myself by making sure I HALT before I continue my journey.

THERE IS A POWERFUL VOICE INSIDE us that has ceaseless wisdom to teach us if only we would listen. The "noise" of society—TV, radio, billboards—along with our hectic lifestyles drowns out our inner voices. Allowing life's noise to keep us from hearing our inner voices is equivalent to having a guru in our home and putting a muzzle on him.

We must unleash our inner sage by turning down the noise. Today, let's enjoy some quiet time. In the silence, we can pray for guidance, wisdom, and serenity. We can let go of stress and worries and let our conscious minds drift. Our goal is to get beneath our surface everyday thoughts to hear the wisdom of our subconscious minds.

Today, turn off the television and radio. Turn on the answering machine for a while. Allow complete silence to enfold you. Soft music or guided imagery tapes are allowed if they help you meditate. Otherwise, silence is preferred. *Shhh.* Do you hear something? It's your inner voice coming through loud and clear.

I listen to my inner voice and open myself to a world of fresh ideas.

WE CAN'T ACCOMPLISH EVERYTHING at once so we must choose what's important to us now and devote ourselves to it.

Here's an exercise to help you discover your priorities. Make a list of what you value. Then ask yourself: Does my list of values match where I'm applying my time and energy? If you say raising well-adjusted children is a priority, are you spending enough time with them? Do you read to them? Do you listen to them? If advancing in your career is important, are you willing to work late, come in early, and go a step beyond what you have been asked to do? Where is your focus?

If your list of priorities matches your actions, congratulations. If your list does not match, you have two choices to alleviate the conflict. You can either redefine your priorities or you can change your behavior to concentrate on what matters most. You can give up those things you now realize don't have value for you. Let go of stalled relationships and unproductive activities.

Scattering our energies on too many projects weakens our abilities. We are capable of achieving so much, but only if we focus.

I concentrate on my priorities and eliminate habits that keep me from focusing on what is important.

Dysfunctional Families *February 26*

TO IDENTIFY DYSFUNCTIONAL BEHAVior, it is helpful to review these four categories: rules, roles, feelings, and communication.

Healthy families have rules that are flexible, and allow their members to be themselves. Dysfunctional families operate under rules like "Don't Talk," "Don't Feel," and "Don't Think for Yourself" that leave members feeling confused and frustrated.

Healthy families have roles that change when the people change. In dysfunctional families, people cannot change roles because one person's change causes a shift in the entire faulty system, and that's not acceptable.

People in healthy families acknowledge and accept all their feelings. Men can cry and women can be angry. People in dysfunctional families minimize, rationalize, and deny their feelings. Or they assign certain feelings to certain family members. For example, the alcoholic might be the only person in the family who can be angry; everyone else must repress their hostilities.

In healthy families, people communicate with each other. Dysfunctional families keep secrets. Healthy families encourage honesty and openness.

I practice healthy habits with regard to rules, roles, feelings, and communication.

"Don't Talk" Rule — February 27

THE "DON'T TALK" RULE MIGHT SOUND like: "Don't put your business on the street" or "Don't dishonor the family." This rule keeps family members from telling what's going on in the family. If we follow the rule and keep the secret, we grow up unsure of ourselves. We grow up afraid to address the issues we will face as adults.

Talking is not a sign of weakness. Talking is not a sign of indiscretion. We can be discriminating in choosing with whom we discuss our personal problems. We don't need to gossip.

But, if we have something on our minds, we have every right to discuss it. We can talk about our fears, worries, what makes us angry, what we love. We can talk about sex, politics, and religion. Talk to family members, friends, co-workers, church members. If you can't talk to any of those people, hire a therapist—a professional listener. Talking about our issues is part of healing ourselves.

We have to get past the "Don't Talk" rule. We can talk and we *must* talk.

I am free to talk about whatever I choose.

Teach Your Children Well *February 28*

When you're young and someone tells you what you are and shows you how to be proud, you've got a head start.

—VIKKI CARR

MANY OF US GREW UP WITH THE IDEA that children should be seen and not heard, but we don't have to carry on this abusive practice. We can treat our children with dignity and respect. Children have the right to think for themselves and to learn from their mistakes. They have the right to discover who they are.

We can help our children find their way by teaching them about the great people from whom they are descended. Share with them the histories of their forefathers and foremothers. Tell them about the heroic, wise, and loving people they were born from. Take them to a library or museum to educate them about our people. One of the most important things we can do is teach our children to be proud of themselves.

I respect young people's strengths and talents and make an effort to give the next generation a chance to learn who they are.

Growth *February 29*

OUR NUMBERS ARE GROWING, changing the fashion, music, food, language, and style of the predominant culture. As our population grows, so does our opportunity to continue to improve the system. Let's prepare ourselves for the time when people of color are the majority in the United States. More and more we are being called upon to lead not only our communities, but the country. Are we ready for the responsibilities of a new age?

The backgrounds of people of color have much in common, but also many differences. We should learn about each other's spirituality, philosophy, and history. The more we understand each other, the better we can work together.

By definition, growth means expansion—moving beyond what's been comfortable. We must expand our minds, widen our focus. Break free of limited thought patterns that hold us back. We should allow ourselves to experience as many different things as we can. We grow through taking risks and exposing ourselves to new environments, fresh information, and different people.

I emancipate myself from self-defeating behavior. I know my freedom is essential to my growth and the growth of the country.

No Excuses — *March 1*

If I became an alcoholic, it is because I failed to take responsibility for my genetic predisposition to alcoholism. It is not my parents' responsibility because they may have been alcoholic. I chose to drink. —JOHN DAVID MENDOZA BRODEUR

NO MATTER WHAT OUR BACKGROUND, no matter what has happened to us, there are no excuses for our behavior today. *We* are solely responsible for our actions and our choices.

Today, let's make a decision to eradicate excuses from our vocabulary. No rationalizing, justifying, or explaining is allowed today, only accepting responsibility for who and where we are.

I am accountable for my actions.

WHAT MOTIVATES US? WHAT DRIVES our actions? Often we give one reason for our behavior when it is really something else. Too many people just accept their lot in life and don't ask questions. But without awareness of the cause, it's impossible to change the effect. To heal and grow, we must review our motives and ask ourselves why we *really* do the things we do.

Here are some examples: A mother keeps her child close to her, saying it's for his protection, and that she loves him. Perhaps the truth is that she feels lonely. A man avoids commitment, saying there are too many available women to devote himself to just one. Perhaps he's really afraid of being abandoned.

It's typical for children to respond with "I don't know" when asked why they left their little brother at the playground or tied the cat's tail to a chair. If we encourage them to be honest about their feelings, they'll tell us the real reason why they did such things. Giving them space to share their jealousy and anger will help them know and understand themselves as they grow. It will help them become complete adults.

Today, let's take the time to learn what motivates our behavior. It will mean all the difference in the final outcome.

I am motivated by healthy, loving principles.

Clear Thinking *March 3*

SPRING CLEANING TIME! SOMETIMES our homes become so cluttered and messy we simply can't take it any more, and we have to do some deep cleaning. Our *minds* also need a good cleaning out from time to time. We have to clear out the cobwebs of damning messages and lay down a polish of affirming thoughts. Clutter hampers our thought processes and confuses us. We can think more clearly when we get rid of old tapes that play negative messages about ourselves.

Clear thinking leads to healthier choices, and therefore, better results. Today, let's make a commitment to get rid of negative thoughts and beliefs so we can head into spring with clear minds and loving hearts.

I clear my mind of debris and noise and create space for healing.

Say Yes to Yourself *March 4*

SAY YES TO YOURSELF. AFFIRM YOURself, your life, your goals, your desires, your dreams. Yes, I deserve a healthy relationship, satisfying work, and a meaningful spiritual life. Yes, I am able to meet my goals. Yes, I am capable of achieving my dreams. Yes! I know. Yes! I can. Yes! I will. Yes! I choose. Yes! I understand. Yes! I do. Yes! I am.

Part of saying yes to yourself might mean saying no to others. These are some things you might say no to so you can affirm yourself: No, I won't be able to join you tonight. No, I really don't want to see that movie. No, I don't agree with you. No, I don't like that. No, I don't choose that. No, I won't.

You can even put the two together: "No, I won't go with you to the movies. (Yes) I want to stay home and study." "No, I don't agree with your opinion. (Yes) This is what I think ..."

It is our right to do what we need to do to take care of ourselves. Make the best choices you can. Say yes to that which works for you and no to that which doesn't.

I say yes to myself and do what is right for me. I allow others to say yes to themselves, even if that means saying no to me.

Pamper Day *March 5*

WE ARE HARDWORKING, RE-sponsible people and sometimes we forget to have fun. Pamper Days are days we give ourselves permission to play or rest or do whatever we want.

Today, think of the most decadent, self-indulgent, wickedly impulsive thing you can do, then do it. Spend the day in bed. Take a long bath. Eat ice cream from the carton. Eat breakfast on the porch. Watch cartoons. Get a massage, facial, manicure, or make-over. Read a "trashy" novel. Or take a long walk, with no destination in mind.

Let's allow ourselves to lighten our load. Jobs, kids, and marriages are important to us and require much time and energy. But we can still take a day to pamper ourselves.

I have the right not only to treat myself well, but to treat myself very *well.*

Self-Talk *March 6*

HAVE YOU EVER LISTENED—I MEAN *really l*istened—to the talk that goes on in your head? When we feel positive, self-confident, and happy, the voices sound like a church choir singing our praises or a squad of cheerleaders rooting us on to victory. When we're feeling insecure or slighted, the dialogue may sound like that popular team of movie critics on TV: Nothing we say or do is right. Or it may sound like the mother that criticized, the father that ignored, or the siblings that teased.

How we talk to ourselves is more important than how anyone else does. If we aren't feeling as confident as we'd like, perhaps it's because of the things we are saying to ourselves.

A good way to become aware of your self-talk is to keep a journal—write down what you are feeling and the thoughts that go with your emotions. Review the messages daily and try to find any patterns and determine if you want to change anything. Once you know what you want to change, you can practice giving yourself better messages. When you hear yourself begin with, "Who do I think I'm kidding? I can't do that." Say "Stop!" out loud if possible. Then tell yourself, "I *can* do this."

I talk to myself with love, respect, and gentleness.

Religion or Spirituality *March 7*

We learned that what's important is not what religion you practice, but believing in what you've been taught.

—ROSE MARY BARSTOW

RELIGION IS BASED ON DOGMA and a structured pattern of worship. Spirituality is more about the feeling about God, nature, our fellows, and ourselves. If we go to church or temple every week, but don't practice the principles behind our religion, we miss the point.

We are born with a spiritual nature—a soul—that demands nourishment just as our bodies require food. "Soul food" could be prayer, song, walking in the woods, or watching children grow—anything that reminds us there is something in this universe bigger than us.

It is your choice whether or not you subscribe to a religion. Buddhism, Christianity, Hinduism, Islam, Judaism, and Christian Science share similar principles and follow the teachings of great masters. Native American and African tribal beliefs offer wisdom about the universe and our places in it. Take faith, hope, guidance, strength, love, and acceptance wherever you find it—in the pages of the Bible, Holy Koran, I Ching, or in the sweat lodge or ceremonial dance.

I am a spiritual being who acts on my beliefs in a way that brings me peace and joy—I deserve it.

Celebrate! *March 8*

WE'VE SURVIVED. THANKS TO OUR grandparents, their grandparents, and their grandparents—we are here. Today, and each day, offers a fresh start, a new time. Let's use it to honor the gifts our people have given us. We can do that by continuing the work done by our elders. We must continue moving forward, trying to make a better place for the next generation.

Let's celebrate the joy we see within our people. Our cultures are rife with merrymaking in dance, song, poetry, and music. Attend a fiesta, luau, powwow, or a "down home" church, and watch us rejoice with abandon. We know how to celebrate!

Let's also reward ourselves for our individual accomplishments. It's healthy to give ourselves a pat on the back once in a while. I'm not talking about being cocky; I'm suggesting we congratulate ourselves at the same time we show gratitude for what we have been able to achieve. The behavior we give attention to is the behavior that gets repeated…so accentuate the positive. This is true for our relationships with others and it's true for ourselves.

I celebrate my beauty and the beauty of my culture with gratitude and love.

AS IN THE REST OF AMERICA, ADDICTIONS run rampant in our communities. Alcoholism and drug abuse typically are what come to mind when we think about addictions and our people.

We also can take normal, healthy parts of life and abuse them to the point of addiction. We can use food to try to escape our feelings, stuffing ourselves in an effort to fill the hole in our souls. Or, we can starve ourselves in a futile attempt to gain a sense of control of our lives.

We also can use people to make us feel good and help us avoid dealing with ourselves. We can become addicted to the "high" that comes with sexual activity and romantic attachment. We can be co-dependent, compulsively focusing on other people's lives instead of our own.

We can even use religion as a means of avoiding our emotions. Churches, temples, and other holy places are not meant to be hiding places. We should go to seek solace, direction, understanding, and fellowship, but not to run from our problems.

Our people have a lot of pain, anger, and grief. If we don't work through these feelings, we are at risk of using substances, activities, or people to avoid them.

I accept my emotions and begin to work through them, rather than trying to escape them through addictive behaviors.

Faulty Thinking *March 10*

The fault of others is easily noticed but that of oneself is difficult to perceive. A man winnows his neighbor's faults like chaff, but his own he hides, as a cheat hides the false die from the gambler.
—BUDDHA

SOMETIMES IT'S EASY TO SEE EVERYone's faults but our own. We can see how this person needs to be more assertive, that person needs to exercise more, the other person needs to learn to listen, and another one shouldn't be so naive.

This is faulty thinking. The only person I need to focus on is me. We are not responsible for others (except our children, and they also have the right to think for themselves). We can't fix people. We can't change them. We can't control them. It's not our job. It's not our business.

Observing the behavior of others can be enlightening when we use it to analyze ourselves. Observation can be a way to hold up a mirror to ourselves and determine how we act in similar situations.

The next time we find ourselves telling someone else how to solve their problems, perhaps we should take our own advice.

Without insulting or criticizing myself, I lovingly focus on my issues today and not on the shortcomings of others.

Posture *March 11*

FOR OUR HEALTH AND WELL-BEING IT'S important to maintain good posture. Correct alignment eases breathing, allowing our blood to deliver essential oxygen to organs and muscles. Good posture also helps alleviate aches and pains.

Standing straight, meeting the world face-to-face also transmits a message about our confidence level. People respond better when we look them in the eye. Good posture doesn't mean you have to walk around stiff as a board. Lift your head up, put your shoulders back, stick your chest out, and then relax.

I stand tall and strong and beautiful in the face of God and know that I am blessed.

Nature's Beauty *March 12*

BE OPEN TO THE BEAUTY AROUND YOU. Take a walk in the park, woods, mountains, or on the beach and allow yourself to appreciate the diverse beauty of nature—newly fallen snow; a sunset; or an ancient, gnarled oak.

In the city, look for beauty in architecture, the sounds of the hustle and bustle of the street, a rainbow in an oily puddle in a parking lot. Watch a child's eyes light up as she hurls down a slide at a playground. Doesn't the gentleman on the park bench look like a wise old tree? Aged, withered...and beautiful.

Beauty is all around me. I just have to open my heart to see it.

IT IS ALL RIGHT TO BE ANGRY. WHAT IS unhealthy is to stuff anger (or any emotion) inside and not express it. All emotions come out whether we consciously communicate them or not. It's inappropriate to voice our anger in sideways methods by using the silent treatment or leaving in the middle of an argument. It's definitely inappropriate to vent hostilities with physical violence. If we aren't able to express our anger verbally, we can use other methods: Yell into a pillow, go for a jog, or write a nasty letter. Do something to release the feelings.

Anger turns inward when we don't tell others we are angry or, at least, slam a couple of doors. Have you ever been in a situation where you didn't tell someone how you felt and then spent days kicking yourself for not speaking up? The anger has to go somewhere, and we often feel safer directing it toward ourselves. But it's not safer. Repressed anger leads to depression.

We can assertively, honestly, and diplomatically share our anger with others. We can tell people what they did and how we feel about it. We can ask for what we want to correct the problem. It is as natural for us to feel anger as it is to feel joy. And it's human to express both. Don't stuff your anger—let it out.

It's OK for me to be angry.

Prosperity *March 14*

MANY OF OUR PEOPLE EXPERIence poverty. And those of us who are financially sound may come from poor families. We may know about using the leftovers of someone else's meals to feed our families. We may know the embarrassment of hand-me-down clothes that don't fit.

Because of our cultures' histories of scarcity, we still may be operating under a mind-set that there's not enough to go around. It's time to let go of this old belief. It's blocking us from enjoying all that the universe has to offer us.

Our Creator has provided us with all we need to go forth in the world and has given us the gift of abundance. There is enough love, money, success, and happiness for all to enjoy. Let's not allow our old thinking to keep us from accepting this gift. When we are prosperous, we should accept our good fortune. We deserve prosperity, and we don't have to be ashamed when we achieve it.

As we grow, our definition of prosperity will grow, and we will allow more success into our lives.

I am rich in love, health, and well-being.

Responsibility *March 15*

Life is a responsible activity. —HOWARD THURMAN

IF WE REVIEW OUR PASTS, WE SEE THAT our lives are the sum of our choices. Some might feel threatened or ashamed by that. Others will feel relieved. If events in our lives are shaped by our choices, think of the power that gives us for the future! If we make responsible choices, we will lead more productive lives.

I'm not suggesting we can control life. Tornadoes strike, people die, companies go bankrupt, and other unpredictable events happen. I'm not suggesting that we can control other people. Children throw temper tantrums, spouses burn dinner, and friends move away. That's life.

But we can control ourselves. We can choose to stay or to go, to remain married or to get a divorce, to quit our job or to ask for a promotion. We shape our lives through responsible activities.

They say that with freedom comes responsibility. The reverse is also true: With responsibility comes freedom.

I pray for guidance and wisdom to live responsibly today and every day. Each day adds up to a lifetime.

TCB

March 16

TCB MEANS "TAKING CARE OF BUSINESS." Doing what needs to be done. This phrase applies to more than just work. We take care of business when we support ourselves financially instead of depending on others. We take care of business when we raise our children to respect and value themselves and others.

Taking care of business doesn't have to be a grim thought. When we take care of business, we take care of ourselves. When we take care of business, we actively participate in our own lives rather than standing by the sidelines watching life pass us by. Think of the words we use to describe our use of time—we can *spend* it or *waste* it. Which would you rather do? Which word implies an assertive choice? Don't let time slip by you; use it wisely. Take care of business.

I lovingly take care of business and take care of me.

Perfectionism *March 17*

On the surface, perfectionism looks like a person is driven to do his or her very best. It's admirable to strive for excellence rather than accept mediocrity. But what actually drives perfectionists is a need to compensate for what they believe is the "truth" about themselves. Perfectionists don't think they are good enough so they spend time and energy trying to "fool" others into believing they are worthwhile people.

We've heard of fashion models who constantly criticize their appearance and millionaires who won't rest until they are billionaires—people always in search of bigger, better, and more.

Perfectionism is a trap that catches us in an impossible game that we can't win—nothing and nobody is perfect. In order to step out of the trap we need to treat the roots of the problem. If you fit the description of a perfectionist, ask yourself: What am I trying to hide?

I release my need to be perfect and accept myself as I am.

LIFE IS PERPLEXING ENOUGH WITHOUT the confusion created by muddled thinking. We need to cleanse our consciousness by removing distractions and getting clear about what we want and the best way to get it. One way to clear the fog from your mind is to write down your goals and stick to the plan. Keep a vision of what you want to achieve in your mind's eye.

Another method of maintaining clarity is to openly and honestly communicate with others. Clear communication eliminates guesswork, saves energy, and guarantees that all parties involved understand what is going on. If both people speak truthfully and directly, there's less chance for assumptions and conjecture.

Know yourself. We only see others as clearly as we see ourselves.

I rid my mind of delusions and illusions.

Dreaming *March 19*

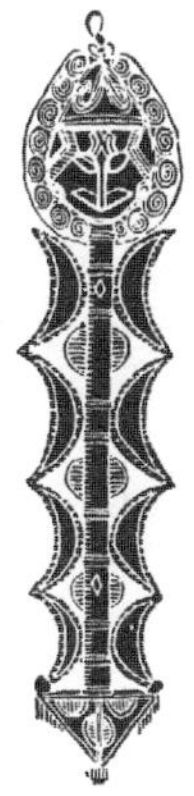

IF WE CAN IMAGINE IT, WE CAN DO IT. EVERY action—every outcome—starts out as an idea. We can allow ourselves to explore our dreams and desires. What do you want to do, be, or have? Make a list for yourself. Pray about it. Dream about it. These are the first steps toward achieving any goal.

Like Martin Luther King Jr. I let my dreams motivate me.

One Day at a Time *March 20*

"ONE DAY AT A TIME" IS A SLOGAN that reminds twelve-steppers to be patient and helps them get through tough times. The recovering alcoholic only has to be sober for this day. The overeater only has to abstain from bingeing for this day.

We can use this philosophy no matter what difficulties we face. We only have today. Focus on getting through today. We can deal with tomorrow when it comes.

We still make plans and set goals. We still save our money to make sure we can pay rent when it is due. One day at a time doesn't mean abusing today without giving thought to tomorrow. One day at a time means using today wisely so we don't have to pay for it tomorrow. One day at a time means enjoying today because tomorrow might not come. One day at a time means allowing ourselves to handle one thought, feeling, activity, decision, or problem at a time. Living one day at a time is simple, pure, and honest.

I appreciate this day because it is the only one I have.

Rebirth *March 21*

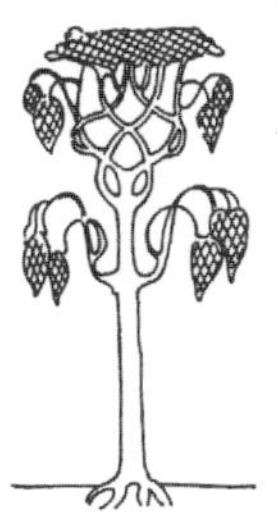

BUDS ON THE TREES, BABY DUCKS AT THE pond, a warm breeze wafts by. Spring is in the air and evidence of nature reinventing itself is all around us. Soon the trees will blossom, and tulips, azaleas, daisies, wildflowers, and poppies will shoot out of the dirt and stretch toward the sun.

The earth dies during winter and waits to be reborn in spring. The change of seasons is just one of the many examples in nature of death leading to a rebirth of something higher and better. The caterpillar must experience the death of its former self to transform into a butterfly. Snakes shed their skin as they grow, leaving behind that which they no longer need. And humans must learn to let go and say good-bye in order to move ahead.

We can take a cue from nature and remake ourselves anew. Each day we have an opportunity to recommit ourselves to all that is loving and life giving. We can allow the warmth of spring to melt our frozen feelings. We can let the lingering daylight shine in our hearts. We can shed useless thoughts from our minds.

With every choice I am reborn.

THE U.S. CONSTITUTION INCLUDES the Bill of Rights, which describes the basic liberties of Americans. The Bill of Rights says we have the right to "life, liberty, and the pursuit of happiness."

We also can create our own individual bill of rights. Some suggestions:

1. We have the right to listen to ourselves.
2. We have the right to express our feelings.
3. We have the right to keep quiet about our feelings if we are not ready to share them.
4. We have the right to say no without explanation, argument, or justification.
5. We have the right to choose our own Higher Power and practice the spiritual discipline that feels right to us.
6. We have the right to know the truth about ourselves and our history.
7. We have the right to privacy and time alone.
8. We have the right to enjoy life.

Add any other ideas you can think of to make this list specific for your needs.

I know my rights and I act on them.

WHY DO TODAY WHAT YOU CAN PUT off until tomorrow? Americans are great at rationalizing procrastination; it's built into our society. It takes ages for a bill to pass through Congress. Community leaders discuss gang violence, teen pregnancy, and illiteracy ad nauseam. After a while, we forget what it's like to get things done.

Let's move past "thinking about it" and "discussing it" to *doing it.* We know right now what tasks have been calling to us for hours, days, months, or years. And, more often than not, we know the exact course of action that needs to be taken. Procrastination is not a matter of indecision—it's a matter of fear. When we are afraid that we'll fail, hurt someone's feelings, look funny, or get into trouble, we don't act.

Use this book and the many other tools available to you to work through your fear. Don't wait until the fear is gone before you make a choice and take action; you'll always be afraid of something. Acting even though we are afraid moves us forward.

I do not let my fear stop me from moving forward. I act with decisiveness and courage.

My grandmother talked to the water. Before we washed, she would tell it how beautiful it was and thank it for cleansing her. —MARY MCDANIEL

WE ALL PROBABLY HAVE FOND memories of grandmothers, grandfathers, mothers, fathers, aunts, and uncles. Our cultures place high value on our ancestors. However, society ignores the knowledge and strength of old people. We don't need to fall into the American trap of disregarding the contributions of senior citizens.

As children, our elders seemed so big and wise. As young adults, we sometimes lose respect for them. Their ways seem old-fashioned, even silly. Who ever heard of talking to the water?

However, when we mature we rediscover the wisdom of our elders. We develop a new admiration for mother's peach cobbler recipe, grandfather's jazz collection, uncle's fishing boat. Older people have so much to teach us. We would be wise to take advantage of one of our greatest resources: our elders.

I explore ways to connect with my elders—whether they're blood relations or not.

STEREOTYPING IS A SIMPLISTIC METHOD of categorizing entire groups by the behavior and characteristics of a few of their members. Whatever traits are available to the human family are shared by all human beings. So some of our people are leaders, teachers, caregivers, providers, healers, and seekers, just as some of us are drunkards, bums, cheats, rapists, liars, and thieves. No person is perfect, therefore no group of people is perfect.

People use stereotypes to hold others down and keep them in boxes. Even so-called compliments (and there aren't many) such as "blacks have rhythm," "Asians are smart," "Latins are lovers," and "Indians are spiritual" can be condescending and belittling. Certainly, we have the right to be proud of the strengths inherent in our cultures. But let's not forget that we are no more and no less than our brothers and sisters. Don't buy into stereotypes—neither those that flatter nor those that fault.

I am a human being, not a stereotype, therefore I am capable of all that is human.

Be Assertive *March 26*

Assertiveness is standing up for ourselves and what we know to be true. It means not allowing others to denigrate or take advantage of us. We have the right to protect our boundaries and reject inappropriate behavior.

There is a difference between assertiveness and aggressiveness. Assertion is confidently making our needs, opinions, and feelings known while being aware that we can't control others. Aggression is demanding, ordering, and pushing to get what we want, acting with an illusion of control.

Practice being assertive. Refuse to let a sales clerk intimidate you into buying clothes you don't want or need. Don't accept the small table in the dimly lit, cramped corner of the restaurant. To do so is to accept abuse. We don't have to tolerate abuse from the culture, our families, or ourselves. Be honest. Be firm. Be confident. Be assertive.

I assert myself because I know I deserve to be treated with respect and kindness.

Faith *March 27*

And we kept faith—faith in God, in our President, and in our country. It was this faith that maintained our hope that someday our dreams would come true, and today they have.

—EVERETT ÁLVAREZ JR.

LIEUTENANT COMMANDER ÁLVAREZ was held captive in Vietnam for 3,103 days. When he was released, he wasn't bitter or vengeful. He was grateful and talked of faith.

Sometimes we are held captive by fear and insecurity. Our journey feels too long; the destination seems hidden behind swirling clouds of mist. We are tired. Like Lieutenant Commander Álvarez, we too can keep the faith. Whenever we feel lost, we can ask God to shed light on our paths. We can trust that we will once again know the way. The fog will lift. We will get through the dark crossings.

Don't give up. Trust God. Trust yourself. You're doing fine.

I walk my path in faith.

Criticism *March 28*

MANY OF US HAVE STRONG INNER critics that tell us when we are wrong. Faultfinding and blame don't help us better ourselves or correct our errors. However, that critical voice is beneficial when we use it to remedy inappropriate behavior.

Here are three steps to help turn the hypercritical judge into a constructive advice giver:

1. Tell the truth. Take an inventory of your actions to determine if you are trying as hard as you can. If you're not truly living up to your potential, let the critic move you in the right direction.
2. Question the critic's motive. Does the critic have your best interests at heart? If so, listen. If not, tell the critic to be quiet.
3. Be fair. If you're not walking the straight and narrow, there's a kind way to get yourself back on track. You don't need to be harsh or rude with yourself. You can firmly, yet gently, correct yourself.

I listen to my inner critic to decipher its message.

Right Attitude *March 29*

I feel that the essence of spiritual practice is your attitude toward others. When you have a pure, sincere motivation, then you have right attitude toward others based on kindness, compassion, love, and respect. —THE DALAI LAMA

OUR ATTITUDES AND PERCEPTIONS shape everything about our lives, including our relationships and our behavior.

Right attitude is knowing that *we* are responsible for our feelings. Our lovers, children, parents, bosses, or friends do not control how we feel. Right attitude is taking care of ourselves and expecting others to take care of themselves. Right attitude is giving freely, wanting nothing in return.

The paradox is that once we stop trying to get and focus on giving, we receive what we never would through manipulation, control, or deceit. When we operate with right attitude, we operate from a spiritual base. Some of the most "religious" folks are also the most judgmental, critical, and faultfinding. If we want to be truly spiritual people, we need to treat our fellow human beings with gentleness and love.

I know what motivates me and I operate with right attitude.

Amends *March 30*

STEPS EIGHT AND NINE IN THE Twelve Steps of Alcoholics Anonymous focus on making amends. Making amends is different from apologizing. We apologize to let the other person know we are aware that we did damage and we are sorry for it. We can apologize for our mistakes a million times, but unless we change our behavior, apologies are meaningless. When we make amends, we mend our ways to make sure we don't make the same mistake again.

Making amends is important for us because it helps us take responsibility for our actions and relieves us of guilt. Holding on to guilt from the past causes excessive self-blame, guilt, and shame. It makes it impossible for us to forgive ourselves. And the ability to forgive ourselves is necessary to being able to forgive others. When we forgive ourselves for our faults and mistakes, it helps us be more tolerant and less judgmental of other people's indiscretions.

When we apologize and make amends with a sincere desire to be forgiven, we can move forward.

Now is the time I take responsibility for my actions. What behavior do I need to amend?

WAITING
I don't want to wait / for fate, / chance, / or divine inspiration. I want to move / Now! / I want to grow / Now!

—CARLEEN BRICE

OBVIOUSLY, WHEN I STARTED "WAITing" I felt very frustrated and impatient. I tend to be an overachiever who has a hard time accepting things as they are. That particular day, I was expecting myself to be in a place that I hadn't yet arrived. It was like expecting a package to arrive in another part of the country when I hadn't mailed it yet.

What I learned by writing this poem was that the future comes in its own time and on its own terms. In the years since I wrote "Waiting" I've realized that the future comes with each passing day. Our next thought is our future. Each day we can do something to prepare ourselves for the next day and the next.

There is never a final destination. When we achieve one goal, it's time to work toward another. When we learn one lesson, a teacher arrives to teach us something else. If we always put our best foot forward, we will always move ahead.

I calmly walk through life with the knowledge that when I am ready, I will learn what I need to know.

Fun — *April 1*

Life's too short and too precious to not be fun. Life is meant to be enjoyed.

—BILLY MELTON

EVEN IF WE LIVE TO BE ONE HUNDRED, we really don't have much time on this planet. So let's make it count. Let's have some fun today! Dance around the bedroom in your underwear; skip rocks across a pond; eat popcorn and candy for dinner; tell silly jokes and laugh out loud; wiggle your toes in the grass; play tag; drive to a secluded spot and watch the sunset; belly dance; go fly a kite; buy or pick fresh flowers; go to a ball game and yell with the cheerleaders; the list of fun things to do is endless.

We all have obligations and responsibilities, but if we look hard enough, we will find a spare hour to spend on amusement. If spending time on pure pleasure makes you feel guilty, remind yourself about the health benefits of fun. Having fun relieves stress and makes us healthier. People have even written books about laughter curing illnesses. . . . Fun is serious business.

Having fun is not wasting time. Having fun is living.

Avoiding Negative People *April 2*

SOMETIMES WE'LL BE ON A ROLL. OUR work will be going well. Our relationships will be fulfilling. And, we're genuinely content with life. Then we encounter one of the "negatives": the complainers, whiners, criticizers, gripers. These people always have a beef. And they aren't satisfied until those around them are just as unhappy as they are. Misery loves company.

If our loved ones need an occasional shoulder to cry on, or if they just want to vent a grief, that's acceptable. But if folks aren't able to move on—if all discussions with them are negative—we don't have to partake. We can set boundaries with friends and tell them we don't appreciate negative diatribes. And if they continue to approach us with unpleasant business, we can eliminate them from our lives. We do not have to tolerate negative people. As a matter of fact, we should avoid them at all costs.

When depressing people come your way, run for your life! Go the other direction, hang up the phone, change the subject, close the door, ignore them...do whatever you can to escape their pessimism.

I protect myself by avoiding negativity.

MOVIES, MAGAZINES, AND COMMERcials try to convince us that happiness can be bought in the form of lavish furnishings, designer fashions, expensive cars, or the "right" mouthwash. If we believe this illusion, we waste precious time and money searching for happiness in places it doesn't exist. We probably also suffer the emptiness and disillusionment that come from looking for the pot of gold at the end of the rainbow.

Well-meaning friends, family members, and clergypeople also may offer magic potions for happiness. They may tell us we'll be happy when we get married, when we graduate, when we get promoted, win the lottery, or go to Heaven. They are partially right; it does feel good to be in relationship with others. And it is wonderful to accomplish a goal. However, we don't have to wait for something to make us happy. We can be happy now. It might help if we change our definition of happiness from instant gratification to contentment and joy. Happiness comes from acting in alignment with our true purpose in life. When we are doing what we came here to do, when we are giving what we are meant to give, then we will find meaning, fulfillment, and satisfaction.

I no longer wait for happiness. I take pleasure in my life now.

HAPPINESS AND SADNESS ARE TWO sides of the same coin—the yin and yang of emotions. While we are more inclined to express cheerful feelings than distressing ones, we must allow ourselves to feel both in order to be complete. Denying our sadness gives us the illusion of controlling our pain, but this illusion extracts a steep price. When we stifle our feelings, we become numb and empty...like zombies. To awaken our true selves, we must release our feelings, including sadness.

We can only experience wholeness if we experience the entire spectrum of human emotions. We can't reject our darker emotions without risking our ability to express the brighter sides of ourselves. When we learn to accept our sadness, we can more easily accept happiness.

Tears are so healing; they are the body's way of cleansing away misery. It's documented that our tears are chemically different when we cry from sorrow than when we cry from laughter. So cry if you need to. Get it out. Let go of the sadness so you can make room for joy. We can't afford the cost of denying the reality of our feelings.

Today's tears clear the way for tomorrow's smiles.

Ah Hah! *April 5*

HAVING AN AWARENESS IS THE FIRST step toward growth. It's when the lightbulb flashes in your mind and you instinctively slap your forehead and say "I get it!"

We can't rush the awareness. It comes when we are ready to understand it. It's frustrating because we want to hurry and change and grow and be our perfect wonderful selves now. Slow down. We already are our perfect wonderful selves. The "ah hahs!" will come. It's part of the process and we can trust it.

We also can't *make* our loved ones or support-group partners "get it" until they are ready. Illumination will come to them when they are prepared to handle it. We can stop trying to force wisdom. We can trust that when we are ready, the teacher will appear.

I trust the growth process and allow myself to enjoy the awarenesses I have made to date, knowing there is always more knowledge to come.

Struggle *April 6*

If there is no struggle, there is no progress.

—FREDERICK DOUGLASS

IMPROVING OUR CHARACTER IS hard work. Recovering alcoholics often say they had to "hit bottom" before they were willing to get help to stop drinking. The same can be said for those of us who spend, work, eat, or play too much. Sometimes we have to suffer the consequences of our behavior before we admit that we need to change.

We can learn a great deal from pain. That's why it's important to accept our mistakes. They are valuable growth opportunities. Have you ever watched a child piece together a puzzle? He or she will stick a piece in one part and then another and another and another, until the part fits. Children learn through trial and error; so do adults.

Progress can feel like a struggle. If the strain begins to wear us down, we can remember that we are benefitting from the process. Do something to lift your spirits (watch a funny movie, play catch with the dog, bake chocolate chip cookies). The struggle will end. There will be better days.

If I am going through a hard time today, I remind myself that this too shall pass.

Expectations of Self *April 7*

CASE STUDIES HAVE SHOWN THAT children perform according to the expectation levels of their teachers. If teachers set high standards for their students, the students try harder and accomplish more. Adults respond similarly. If supervisors and spouses demonstrate confidence and trust in our abilities, we do all we can to meet their expectations.

Our inner thinking also guides our performance level. If we believe we are capable of excellence, we stand a far greater chance of achieving it. If we have low expectations of ourselves, our achievements will match. We can treat the inner child in us like a good teacher would treat a student: Convey faith in ourselves. We can ask ourselves to reach higher, stretch farther, and be better. We can act with the assumption that we have whatever it takes to achieve our goals.

We can require positive responses in ourselves and still be realistic about our limitations. Don't expect yourself to get an A on a test without studying or to master computer programming after one lesson.

Prepare yourself then execute.

I think highly of myself and achieve my goals with ease.

You Are Unique *April 8*

WITH MORE THAN FIVE BILLION people in the world, it's hard to believe that there are no two people exactly alike. No two individuals—not even twins—look, think, move, speak, and dream exactly alike. But after all, God's imagination is powerful enough to create innumerable forms of life…why not billions of original people?

What is it that makes us unique? Is it our DNA, our experiences, the way the planets were aligned when we were born? I'm going to suggest it is the essence of our artful Creator living in each and every one of us that, when combined with our upbringing and heritage, makes us unique.

Let's appreciate our specialness by discovering our unique talents and contributing them to the world. Baking cakes, making folks laugh, leading others in the right direction, knowing just when to offer a kind word, or being able to see a statue in a hunk of wood are just a handful of talents that make a person stand apart.

The Great Spirit has given you a combination of talents, insights, and ideas that no one else in the world has. Do you know what they are?

I share all that is uniquely me.

Flexibility *April 9*

WE CAN'T BE SO DEEPLY ROOTED IN our beliefs that we are unable to bow to the winds of change. When presented with a fresh idea, a better way, an unusual perspective, we must be flexible enough to decide if this new information is helpful. We can't benefit from what other people offer if we are too rigid to listen.

There is strength in flexibility. Think of suspension bridges that support tons of weight, yet sway when rocked by earthquakes. We can more easily bear life's tremors if we don't stiffen our minds with limiting beliefs. As Judo and Karate students are aware, relaxing into a fall eases the pain and lessens the chance of being injured. We don't have to agree with everything we hear or read, but there even can be kernels of truth buried within arguments we don't believe in. We should develop a receptive attitude and be willing to consider other people's views.

Like the bridge that weathers a quake, let life shake you up a bit. That's how we grow.

I stretch my mind and increase my intellectual flexibility.

LIFE IS FULL OF MANY LOSSES—MOVING, divorce, death, illness, being fired. We even can experience happy occurrences as losses—getting married means the loss of our old "swinging single" days; getting a new job may mean losing association with well-liked co-workers.

With loss and change comes grief. We may not grieve as hard or as much over moving to a new home as over the death of a loved one, but we *will* grieve. When we change, we have to let go of a part of ourselves. Sometimes temporarily, sometimes permanently, we experience a shift in our self-image. And we may have to mourn this loss of identity.

Grief is an essential part of the growth process. It's the beginning of letting go and moving on to new opportunities. When we grieve, we heal and learn from the process. Whatever losses you have experienced, allow yourself to grieve.

Grieving is part of healing and growth.

Hope *April 11*

OUR EXPERIENCES WITH HOPE IN THIS country have been different. Many Chinese, Japanese, Korean, Mexican, Cuban, and other immigrants came to *Gum Shan* ("the Mountain of Gold," which is what Chinese immigrants called America) specifically because of their hope of building a better life. And many—like Dr. Shih mai-ye, the first Chinese woman to graduate from an American medical school; Daniel Ken Inouye, the first Japanese-American elected to the U.S. Congress; and Dr. José Julio Henna, a Puerto Rican immigrant who founded New York City's French Hospital—realized their dreams but probably not without experiencing prejudice.

Africans had their hopes stripped from them before their feet hit the shore. Native Americans had their hopes for peaceably sharing their country dashed by greedy, soulless people. But like other disadvantaged people, African-Americans and Native Americans have been able to reach deep inside themselves, find a place of confidence and faith, and meet their goals. The people of color who make it are the ones who don't let discrimination destroy their hope, which Jesse Jackson acknowledges in his call for us to "keep hope alive."

I believe in myself and trust that my Grandfather, the Great Spirit, will help me fulfill my deepest desires.

ONE WAY THAT ABUSED PEOPLE PROtect themselves is to cut themselves off from their feelings. We deny, minimize, stuff, avoid, and "forget" feelings. After being disconnected from our emotions for so long, it can be hard to determine how we feel. We may be able to say we feel good or bad but know no other words to describe our emotions. If you are having trouble identifying your feelings, this list of adjectives might help. Do you feel: abandoned, abused, accepted, affectionate, afraid, bewildered, brave, brokenhearted, beaten, beautiful, caged, calm, comfortable, compassionate, compulsive, confident, confused, deserving, different, dirty, domineering, dumb, egocentric, embarrassed, enslaved, equal, evil, excited, feminine, frigid, frustrated, gutless, grateful, hateful, helpful, hopeful, horny, insecure, inspired, jealous, judgmental, kicked around, lazy, loving, masculine, misunderstood, needed, optimistic, paranoid, powerless, proud, rejected, resentful, rewarded, sadistic, secure, self-assured, tender, tired, ugly, unequal, useless, victimized, violent, warm, or weary?

This is just a fraction of all the words to relate how you feel. Amazing isn't it?

I use specific language to describe my feelings. I express myself clearly and effectively.

Wholeness *April 13*

A LEGACY OF RACISM IS A FEELING of incompleteness that many of us have. We've been taught that we are somehow lesser than or substandard to whites. This feeling of inadequacy can lead us to liquor, lovers, or pills to make us feel better. Or we may overcompensate because we feel we have something to prove. We don't have to work harder, run faster, or smile wider to convince anybody that we are competent. We are just fine as we are. Nobody can make us feel inferior unless we let them. When we maintain our center, our balance, we can better handle prejudicial forces that try to negate our worth. Today, let's visualize ourselves coming full circle.

The circle is a universal archetype for wholeness. In Native American spirituality, the circle appears as a medicine wheel—a tool of growth and creation that increases power, offers growth experiences, and raises awareness. In Chinese cosmology, we find the circle as the yin/yang symbol. Even Carl Jung used a mandala, the Sanskrit word for circle, to symbolize the self.

We are whole. We are complete. Reach back into your ancestral experiences—before you were taught otherwise—and remember.

I am whole and complete exactly as I am.

Owning Our Power *April 14*

WHAT WE TYPICALLY THINK OF WHEN we hear the word power is having fame and fortune or being able to wield authority over other people. Real power is the physical, mental, or spiritual ability to act or produce an effect.

From the janitor to the CEO, all of us have such power. Our Creator has endowed us with fortitude. Think of Sojourner Truth's acknowledgment of her power in her "Ain't I a Woman?" speech. She talked about the trials and tribulations she had suffered in her life and the strength with which she had faced them. In giving her opinion, she was able to demonstrate the hypocrisy in the arguments against allowing women equal rights. Here she was in 1851—a black woman, a slave—owning her power by giving momentum to the suffrage movement.

We, too, can acknowledge our capabilities and strengths. We own our power when we stop acting as victims and take responsibility for our lives. We don't need to ask others to do for us what we can do for ourselves. Whatever we want to improve, we can do it.

I own my power as a child of God. I have the ability to do marvelous things.

Storytelling *April 15*

Stories are medicine. —CLARISSA PINKOLA ESTÉS

OUR CULTURES HAVE RICH ORAL TRAditions. We tell stories to entertain, instruct, and pass along family history. Storytelling is also part of the recovery process. People in therapy or support groups spend time sharing their histories to help them discover their motivations and behavior patterns.

If we have been psychologically wounded, we can help heal ourselves by telling our stories to safe, supportive people. We can share our feelings with others who have experienced the same trauma that we have. We can confess the damage we have done to others, and the damage we have inflicted on ourselves.

Telling our *cuentos* has a recuperative power, and we may need to tell them over and over again to fully reap the benefits.

I share my story with others and take another step toward health.

Alone or Lonely *April 16*

BEING ALONE IS DIFFERENT FROM BEING lonely. Part of spirituality is spending time in solitude. We take time to hear ourselves think, listen to our hearts beat, and get in tune with our higher selves. When we can enjoy our time alone, knowing that silence and solitude contribute to our growth, we have high self-esteem.

If we must always be around others or live with the noise of the television or stereo, maybe we are afraid of being alone. To people who aren't at home with themselves, silence can be threatening.

It's normal to feel lonely from time to time. We are social beings and need to spend time with others. But if we aren't centered, we can feel alone in a crowded room. We can alleviate some of our loneliness if we spend time getting to know and like ourselves. We also can ease our fears by acknowledging that we are never alone. The loved ones who have passed on are always with us. Our Creator is always with us.

I give myself the precious gift of solitude without fear of being alone.

Go with the Flow *April 17*

IMAGINE YOURSELF GENTLY DRIFTING downstream on a river. The sunlight shines through the leaves on the trees, sparkling on the water like diamonds. The only sound you can hear is the sound of the water gurgling over rocks and lapping against the riverbank. It is warm. You are safe. You float along without a care in the world. Easy, isn't it?

As you get farther down the river, clouds begin to block the sun. You shiver a bit and smell rain in the air. You notice you're heading for rapids. You grab a branch and hold on. The water rushes over you, knocking you into the bank. You hit your head on the rocks, but you don't let go of the branch. Rain pours down on you. Thunder crashes and lightning flashes. You are soaked, afraid, and miserable but you hang on and survive the storm. The sky clears and the water calms.

This is the river of life. It's easy to have faith in the good times, but what about the rocky days? Either way, we are being cared for. We can let go and let the river take us where we need to go.

I go with the flow, knowing that I am cared for and protected.

BRIDGES CONNECT TWO PLACES THAT are separated by water, canyons, or other unmanageable terrain. We can create spiritual bridges for ourselves to help us navigate life's complex trails.

When we are feeling isolated, we can use our relationships as a bridge to feeling, once again, like a part of humanity. When we are feeling lost, we can visualize where we want to be and build a bridge to take us there. When we are feeling harried, we can use meditation as a bridge to transport us to a tranquil haven. Therapy offers a bridge back to sanity.

Perhaps the most sound bridge is our Maker. Our Higher Power offers us a solid thoroughfare through the steepest peaks and over the most turbulent waters.

We also can serve as bridges to help our fellow travelers cross tough passages. We can listen, support, encourage, defend, and champion them.

I build a bridge from the life I have to the life I want.

Manipulation *April 19*

INFANTS CRY AS A FORM OF COMMUNICATION. Crying is how babies tell their parents they are hungry, wet, or sleepy. Pretty soon, they cry when they are angry or when they want to be held. Babies learn they can get their needs met by crying.

We are adults. Most of us don't require the caretaking or generosity of others to meet our basic needs. If we are hungry, we can make dinner. However, we do need the love and support of others, but we may not know how to get them without manipulation. We may drop hints about what we want or need. We may lay on the guilt—trying to make someone else take responsibility for our feelings.

If we want something, we can be up front and ask for it directly. We can ask for a hug, loan, favor, compliment, surprise, even a present. People respond much better to frank requests than they do to manipulation.

I ask for what I want.

Authority *April 20*

AUTHORITY IS THE POWER TO MAKE decisions in our lives. Sometimes we look to others to save us from our problems. Or we wait for parents, bosses, spouses, or other authority figures to give us authorization to act. We don't need permission from anybody else to act on our own behalf.

If we are unhappy with our lives, we only need to look inside for the wisdom to make changes. That is where our authority lies.

I have the authority to run my life.

Comfort Zones *April 21*

BABIES BEGIN THEIR EMOTIONAL separation from their mothers when they begin to crawl. They venture away from Mom more often and explore the world around them. But if you observe them, you'll see they only go so far. As long as Mother is within sight, they feel protected.

Adults also have "comfort zones" in which we feel safe. We don't like to go outside of this space, because it is scary. Our comfort zone could be a long-held job, neighborhood, relationship, or attitude. We stay in a position, home, or marriage because we feel safe there. We hold on to old beliefs because it is too threatening to change our opinions.

It's scary to take risks; it feels like we're about to jump from the edge of a cliff. But that is where the energy is. That is where growth lies. As children do, we can widen our comfort zones little by little: Seek counseling for a soured relationship, go back to school, visit other places, read materials that challenge your thinking. There's a big, wide world waiting for you outside your comfort zone.

I take a leap of faith and move outside my comfort zone.

THE FIRST STEP TOWARD SOLVING our problems is taking responsibility for our part in them. Our choices contribute to almost every difficulty we face. Why did we choose that job? Why did we leave that relationship? What did we allow? What signs did we ignore? We should analyze our problems to determine our culpability; not to blame, but to learn from our mistakes so we do not repeat them.

If we face a perplexing dilemma today, we can request help in unraveling the riddle. We can pray and meditate to gain strength from the Creator Spirit. We can ask perceptive relatives and friends for their advice. We can seek professional guidance from a therapist, counselor, lawyer, or other authority. We don't have to—and probably shouldn't—make decisions in a vacuum. Plenty of resources are available to help us find solutions. Of course, the final decision is up to us. What does our inner wisdom tell us to do?

With direction, faith, and a little creativity, we can piece together the pieces of life's puzzles.

My problems are opportunities for learning and growth, and I know I have the ability to solve them.

Serenity Prayer *April 23*

God, grant me the serenity to accept the things I cannot change, the courage to change the things I can, and the wisdom to know the difference. —REINHOLD NIEBUHR

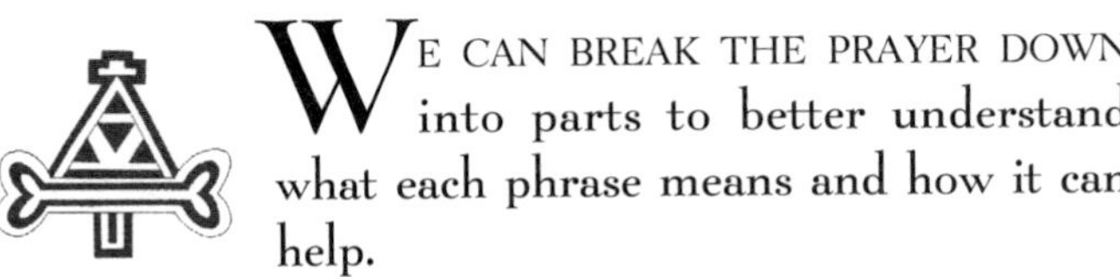

WE CAN BREAK THE PRAYER DOWN into parts to better understand what each phrase means and how it can help.

"God, grant me": Humbly asking for our Higher Power's assistance reminds us that we are human and we have limitations.

"the serenity": With peace of mind comes clarity, and with clarity comes ability to act.

"to accept": If we cannot control something, we must learn to accept it.

"the things I cannot change": There are some things that we can't control.

"the courage": Changing demands bravery and tenacity.

"to change": We ask God to help us transform ourselves, stretch ourselves to be all that we can be.

"the things I can": Our attitudes, behavior, and choices.

"and the wisdom to know the difference": With God's direction, we will know what to do.

The Serenity Prayer helps me find my way.

WE WHO HAVE BEEN IMPRISoned, violated, cheated, and denied feel justified in hating those who actively try to oppress us.

Our world is full of hate—music lyrics, movies, and the evening news deliver images of people fighting and killing out of hatred. Police stations in most major cities even have "hate crime" divisions that monitor racist groups bent on destruction.

Racist, sexist, and other oppressive attitudes are repugnant and loathsome, and we should not accept them. But violence and rage do not lead to positive social change. Love, truth, and honor are powerful forces that no amount of hate can withstand.

Loving your enemies does not mean smiling while a bigot insults you. Loving your enemies means acknowledging that nothing beneficial comes from hatred. Mahatma Gandhi demonstrated that change comes not through hate but through love. Martin Luther King Jr. started his movement hoping to redeem America's soul. Nelson Mandela and Desmond Tutu broke South Africa's system of apartheid using the same principles. Like these great leaders, we can put our hatred aside and fight wrongs.

I unlock my heart and release hatred. With a serene and loving mind, I attack injustice.

Jealousy *April 25*

JEALOUSY IS WHAT WE FEEL WHEN WE are afraid somebody is going to take someone away from us—when we perceive a wealthy man or an intelligent woman as our rival. Children often feel jealous at the birth of a sibling when they realize they will have to share Mommy and Daddy with someone else. They fear their parents don't have enough love to go around.

As adults, sometimes we forget there's enough love, attention, affection, and approval to go around. Our mates can love us and still have deep relationships with others. Our children can have busy lives and still find time for us. When jealousy clouds our vision, we may try to discourage our loved ones from having friendships and activities. If we act on our jealousy—being suspicious, pouting, yelling—we may cause the very thing we fear; we may distance ourselves from those we love.

Just as we can have outside interests and still give priorities to our relationships, so can our families and friends have relationships with other people. Let's lend them the same support we expect for ourselves.

I liberate myself from rivalry and treat my loved ones and myself with trust and respect. There is enough love for us all.

Accepting the Good *April 26*

When you expect good, it's available constantly and it makes itself a reality in your life. —ALFRE WOODARD

SOMETIMES WE GET SO CAUGHT UP IN what is bad or wrong in our lives, we forget what is good. We do have much to appreciate—our relationships and our health to name the most important. And if we are friendless and ill, we can be grateful for a new day in which to remedy our situation.

Many of us may find it hard to allow good into our lives. We may have grown so accustomed to negativity and tribulation that it seems as if good fortune belongs to other people. However, if we make room for good by embracing healthy relationships, accepting satisfying work, and surrounding ourselves with positive people and rewarding opportunities, we will experience the best life has to offer.

With practice and patience, "the good life" will be the only life you know.

I deserve happiness. I open myself to abundance and joy.

Gifts *April 27*

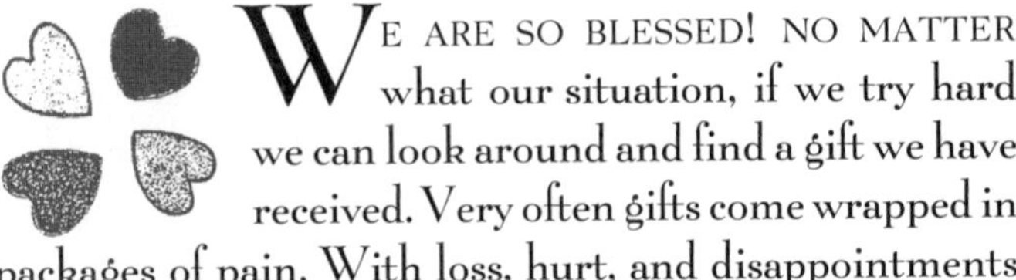

WE ARE SO BLESSED! NO MATTER what our situation, if we try hard we can look around and find a gift we have received. Very often gifts come wrapped in packages of pain. With loss, hurt, and disappointments come valuable lessons; not the least of which is the knowledge that we can survive pain.

Let's be thankful for the benefaction of our Higher Power and demonstrate our gratitude by passing along what we have received. The greatest contribution to the world we can make is to be who we really are. It takes practice thinking of ourselves as gifts to the universe. We need to affirm our special talents and abilities. We need to treat ourselves with consideration and respect. We also should value the endowments of our brothers and sisters—for they, too, play a role in the divine plan.

We each have a mission in life that we can only fulfill if we are being true to ourselves.

I am a valuable part of God's plan. I share my gifts with others with a spirit of gratitude.

Survival — *April 28*

LIFE IS ABOUT MORE THAN SCRAPING BY and earning a living. Life is about enjoyment and purpose and satisfaction. Too often, we get caught up in the day-to-day hustle and miss out on what life has to offer. We go weeks or months or even years before acknowledging we are not happy in a relationship or in our job. We go days or longer without telling our spouse that we love him or her or telling our children they bring joy to our life.

Yes, we must work to put food on the table and keep a roof over our heads. But we also have the choice and the ability to be aware every day that this is our *life.* This may be our only shot at happiness. Life is a precious gift, don't waste it.

I shift my focus from surviving life to living life.

Choosing Thoughts *April 29*

MAKE PEACE WITH YOUR THOUGHTS. Let them be your friends. Let them nurture and help you.

Choose your thoughts as you would choose a friend. Are your thoughts caring, supportive, and inspirational? Do they add to your enjoyment in life? Do they bring you illumination and joy? Do they spur you on to greater heights?

Keep the thoughts that praise, encourage, and uplift you. Relinquish the ones that bring you down, keep you stuck, or give you grief.

I choose my thoughts carefully. My greatest friendship is with myself.

Stay on the Path *April 30*

EACH OF US IS ON A UNIQUE JOURNEY. Society presents many distractions—television, movies, social events—that call out for our attention. Sometimes we veer off track by trying to walk the paths of others. We cannot embark on the journey for our friends and family and they cannot do it for us. There are times when we may travel with others—church members, relatives, support group buddies—and offer each other sustenance and encouragement. But ultimately we must walk alone.

There is no need to explain your method of transportation or justify your destination. Eliminate distractions so you may easily notice the guideposts your Higher Power set up for you. When you need directions, watch for the footprints of the ancestors who have gone before you. Don't get sidetracked. Ignore the detours. Stay on the path. Walk tall.

My path leads me to glorious places!

Lean on Me *May 1*

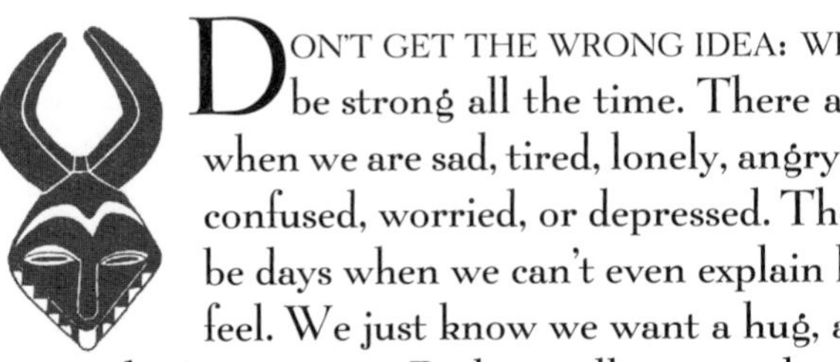

DON'T GET THE WRONG IDEA: WE CAN'T be strong all the time. There are days when we are sad, tired, lonely, angry, afraid, confused, worried, or depressed. There will be days when we can't even explain how we feel. We just know we want a hug, a laugh, or another's presence. Perhaps all we need on these dreary and desperate days is somebody to lean on.

It's natural and healthy to reach out to a friend when we need to lift our spirits. The best friends accept, encourage, nurture, and love us when we feel worthless and hopeless. They remind us that we are beautiful, funny, and smart when we can't see that ourselves.

We do ourselves a wonderful favor when we allow others to help us. Human interaction is good for us physically as well as mentally and emotionally. We also give a great gift to others when we let them be there for us; human connection helps the giver as well as the receiver. We don't have to wait until we're feeling low or weak to call a friend. Like eating fruits and vegetables and getting plenty of exercise, friendship just might be preventative medicine!

I lean on my friends and feel the power of friendship.

Empathy *May 2*

EMPATHY LESSENS THE DISTANCE BEtween us and other people. When we empathize we put ourselves in the other people's shoes—walk a mile in their moccasins, so to speak—and try to understand what it feels like to be them. We leave behind our woes, and beliefs and just listen. We share the feelings of the other person.

Each person is different, and no one will see life exactly as we do. But if we can close off our egocentric mentality and shift our frame of reference, we will find common ground. Perhaps we haven't had the exact same experience as the other person, but if we search our memory, we probably have felt the same way. Maybe we haven't had a lover cheat on us, but a parent abandoned us. We can share the sense of betrayal and distrust with the cuckolded spouse. Maybe we've never been burglarized, but someone peeked in our diary. We can remember feeling violated and better understand the person who has been robbed.

When we get our egos in check, communication is better, and we can effectively help others.

I move outside of myself and view life through the eyes of others, connecting with them and myself.

Baggage *May 3*

WHEN WE GO ON VACATION, WE TRY to pack so that we don't have so much to carry. We know our travels will be more pleasant if we carry a light load. It's the same with life: This is definitely one trip when it's OK to forget your luggage.

The baggage we carry—the hurts, disappointments, regrets, and anger from the past—weighs us down. We do not ease our pain by holding on to grudges. Seeking revenge doesn't take away what happened to us and won't make us feel better. Nobody wins from holding on to the past. Let go of your hurts by telling about those that hurt you. Seek justice instead of revenge. Forgive yourself for missed opportunities.

Let's put our baggage down and experience how it feels to be free of the load. Practice forgiveness. Practice thinking in the here and now. Practice letting go instead of holding on. See how much faster you can ease on down the road?

I can get to my next destination much easier without heavy baggage.

BEFORE A RACE, CONCERT, OR AN IMportant meeting, successful athletes, performers, and business people visualize themselves succeeding at their endeavors. They first envision victory in their mind's eye, which creates a "memory" of being successful, giving them confidence so they can "repeat" the winning behavior. Our minds can't tell the difference between an actual event and an imagined action. Why not put the power of your imagination to work to help you advance through life?

First, find a quiet space and allow yourself to relax. Take ten deep breaths. Hold the air inside for ten seconds and release it slowly. What action do you want to effect? Maybe you want to feel confident when you meet with a client tomorrow morning. Imagine yourself greeting the client with a smile. Picture the conference room and seat yourself comfortably in the chair—back straight, confidently looking him or her in the eye. See yourself in control of the meeting, easily answering all the questions. This same technique will work for other challenges we may face.

Visualization is only one ingredient in the recipe for success. If we have not done the work, visualizing our triumph is foolish. We must be able to deliver the goods.

I picture myself a winner!

CINCO DE MAYO COMMEMORATES THE 1862 battle of Puebla, in which outmanned Mexican troops defeated invading French forces. Mexican-Americans mark the occasion with parades, festivals, speeches, and dances.

As with other ethnic holidays, we are all invited to the party. We can learn more about Mexican culture and share in the celebration. We can all rejoice because we know what it is like to triumph over defeat. We know what it is like to be outnumbered and undersupported and yet flourish. We all have our battles to fight. Today, let's remember that we can win!

No matter what our ethnic backgrounds, we can celebrate the courage and solidarity of Cinco de Mayo.

I honor the tenacity, bravery, and vitality of Mexican-Americans and people everywhere who continue to fight for liberty.

Try Something New *May 6*

MOST OFTEN WE END UP IN RUTS because we are unaware. We do the same things so many times that pretty soon, we can do them without thinking about them. After driving the same way to work day after day, we leave our houses and "come to" when we arrive. It feels as if our cars get there on their own.

We can bring ourselves out of a rut by encouraging ourselves to be aware. One good way to become more alert is to try something new. We have to concentrate more when doing something new. Because we are learning, we have to pay more attention to what we are doing.

Today, we can learn a new recipe, enroll in a class, or take a new route to work—anything to awaken us to the choices we make. We can have fun with our new learning and invite friends and family to participate. Not only will we pull ourselves out of a rut, but we'll have a unique way to spend quality time with the people we love, which in itself might be something new.

I try one new activity and learn about life and myself.

SO MANY OF US WAIT UNTIL LIFE IS really hard before we ask God to intervene. We may feel embarrassed or ashamed to lean on something outside of ourselves. But faith is empowering. We can ask a Higher Power how we should handle even the most minute details.

When we turn to a priest, shaman, Iman, preacher, or grandparent for insight and wisdom, they do not solve our problems for us. They help us find the solutions. When we look inside and get in tune with the universal power inside us, we discover the courage and strength to take on any task.

We can look at our elders and our ancestors and know they survived by trusting their connection to God. Our people have come this far by faith. We, too, will advance with trust in the divine plan for our lives.

My faith is my strongest weapon against adversity. I use it well and often.

THE PERCEPTIONS, EMOTIONS, AND events in our personal lives carry over to our work lives. Whatever unresolved issues we have with ourselves will get acted out in the workplace. So if we have problems with authority figures, we'll hate or fear our supervisor. If we overcompensate with responsibility, we'll be unable to delegate duties to employees. Or if we are distrustful, we'll have difficulty working in teams.

Some work environments are unhealthy and foster low productivity and morale. Managers of such offices probably are acting out their old patterns, causing strife and frustration. If so, we can address the problem. By calling a staff meeting, writing a memo to our boss, or consulting the Human Resources Department or Affirmative Action Officer. If our attempts to correct the situation don't work, we can leave. We have choices about how to handle workplace problems.

Sometimes when we honestly evaluate the situation, we see that the true problem is with ourselves. Perhaps we have settled for a job we are overqualified for. Or we have yielded to racial or sexual harassment. If we find that we are the cause of our discord, we can change the thoughts and behavior patterns that cause problems.

I separate my unresolved issues from my attitudes about work and my job.

MANY OF OUR ANCESTORS WERE taken hostage, exploited, sold, and swindled. Generations of people had no control over where they lived and what type of work they could do. Even small choices that we may take for granted—getting a drink of water, selecting a seat in a movie theater or restaurant—were denied them.

For most of this country's history, people of color were targets for torture and hostility. Physical jeopardy was a lingering threat that caused feelings similar to those of abused children. But to be angry only brought more danger, therefore, many people swallowed their anger and felt the frustration of no control.

But the past is behind us. We can take appropriate control of ourselves. No one can hold us back now. We don't need to (and really can't) try to control people so we can feel safe.

We can't control the perceptions people have of us, but we can control the systems that are arranged to protect us. We can control whom we elect to represent us. We also can control whether or not we believe the stereotypes. Controlling doesn't lead to security and peace of mind. Faith does.

I focus on controlling what I can. I leave the rest to God.

Inferiority *May 10*

The color of the skin makes no difference. What is good and just for one is good and just for the other, and the Great Spirit made all men brothers.

—WHITE SHIELD

THERE IS A LEGACY OF RACISM IN THE United States that tells us to think lowly of ourselves. The longer our kin have lived here, the greater the chance that we will have internalized bigoted opinions about our worth. If we do not think we can achieve, grow, move, or change, we never will. More than any other factor, what we think about ourselves will determine what we do in life.

If we are limiting ourselves with negative thoughts about our value, we can remind ourselves we are all equal in the eyes of the universe. We are not inferior to anybody. We are all brothers and sisters.

I release myself from feelings and thoughts of inferiority. I know my value.

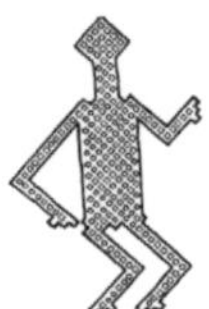

NO MATTER HOW BAD THINGS GOT, our ancestors found something to laugh at. Humor was one of their positive coping skills.

A sense of humor can get us through some pretty tough spots, but sometimes it's hard to find things to laugh at. The bills aren't paid. The house is a mess. We are alone, sick, or tired. We feel like everybody is on our case.

In those times when it's difficult to smile, we can ask for our Higher Power's help. We can let God fill us with enthusiasm so that we can keep going. Think of people who "get happy" in church. The word "enthusiasm" comes from the Greek word *entheos,* which means "to inspire" and *entheos* was derived from *theos,* the Greek word for "God."

We also can look for the twinkle in our mate's eyes or the delight in a child's voice. Feeling connected to others helps lift our spirits and reminds us that we're not alone.

I enthusiastically face the day.

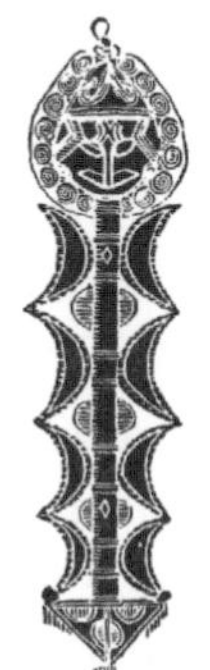

IT IS JUST AS DEVASTATING FOR A LITTLE girl to be taught that she is less valuable than her brothers as it is for a child of color to be taught that he is less valuable than a white child. Women of color take a double hit, with society devaluing our femaleness *and* our ethnicity.

We must rid ourselves of the cancer that divides us and makes us fight. Acrimonious debates about male and female roles only separate us further. Men are not better than women. Women are not better than men. We are all equal human beings, and we all deserve equal treatment in the home, workplace, street, and under the law.

Today, let's honor sisters like Harriet Tubman, Ada Deer, Diana Chang, Rosa Parks, Ying Lee Kelly, Audre Lorde, Nita Gonzales, Norma Aleandro, Kristi Yamaguchi, Joann Tall, and our grandmothers, mothers, sisters, and friends. Let's acknowledge women of color's strength, beauty, intelligence, and power.

I value and respect my sisters and brothers equally.

Caretaking *May 13*

CARETAKING IS WHEN WE TAKE CARE of other people for unhealthy reasons rather than out of genuine concern. Maybe we caretake because we want to feel needed or we want to avoid our issues.

Many of us didn't learn how to take care of ourselves as we grew up. We might have been raised in a large family and had to help care for younger siblings. We might have grown up in a poor family and learned to give away our share of resources to other family members. Many of us were reared in situations that required the effort of all family members sharing and working together. We learned to love and care for one another.

Where that philosophy goes wrong is when we don't also learn to love and care for ourselves. When all we know how to do is give, we set ourselves up to feel resentful. When people need our help, we should give. When we need the assistance of others, we should ask. Mutual caregiving is healthy. However, we aren't responsible for others and we shouldn't act like it. If we have been caretaking those around us, we can learn to let go. We can teach ourselves to set limits for what we will and will not do. We can develop our own characters and leave others to do the same.

I stop taking care of people and start giving care. I also allow myself to receive the support of others.

Self-Confidence *May 14*

If you have no confidence in self you are twice defeated in the race of life. With confidence you have won even before you have started. —MARCUS GARVEY

WE ARE NOT SLAVES. WE ARE NOT AT the mercy of the master or the boss. We own ourselves. Our lives are ours to do with what we wish. We are free to make our own decisions and live by their consequences.

If we have been irresponsible or prone to procrastination, we lose credibility with ourselves. If our actions have taught us that we'll give up or fail, how can we trust that today will be different? By following through. Select a task and write it down, even if it is something simple like remembering to buy a loaf of bread. Then do it. And do the same tomorrow. We can boost our self-confidence by building our credibility. With practice, we will learn that we can trust ourselves to come through.

To help us be more certain of our capacities for achievement, we can look at the accomplishments of people like Crowfoot, Phillis Wheatley, Wing F. Ong, Henry B. Gonzáles, Patsy Takemoto Mink, José Torres, and Black Hawk. We can share the same conviction in ourselves as they did in themselves.

I trust myself to follow through.

MANY OF US DON'T KNOW WHAT TO do when people ask us to do something we don't want to do. We worry about being impolite, selfish, or cruel if we decline. We wonder if they will still like us. We make up excuses or tell fibs to get out of the situation. Our stories may keep us from doing the dreaded deed, but we still don't feel right. We feel guilty and ashamed telling lies or avoiding people. It's a no-win situation. Either we end up agreeing to something we disagree with, or we tell a lie. But there is another solution.

We can just say no.

We don't have to justify or rationalize or explain. We needn't worry about being discourteous or hurting the other person's feelings. If we want to say no, that is our right. We have the right to do what we want and not do what we don't want. We have the right to disagree or dislike.

We don't have to shout or frown to get our point across. We can kindly, sincerely—yet, firmly—say how we feel.

I say no when I want to. It is my prerogative.

:: :: :: :: :: :: :: :: :: :: :: :: :: :: :: :: ::

Giving Support *May 16*

WE CAN'T EXPECT TO GET WHAT WE aren't willing to give. Many of the ideas in this book are about focusing on our needs and getting what we desire. However, we shouldn't concentrate so much on ourselves that we neglect those we love. If we reflect on what our friends and families need from us, we'll probably realize they are the same things we need from them: encouragement, understanding, respect, attention, and compassion.

Of course, the easiest way to find out what folks want is to ask. We can start a dialogue with our friends and invite them to tell us their hopes, dreams, fears, and desires. We can share our wishes with them and make a pact to support each other. If we have a mutual goal—losing weight, finishing school, finding a new job—we can work as partners to achieve it.

It could be that our loved ones have told us what they needed, but we just haven't been listening. Let's show our brothers and sisters that we care by hearing their pleas for assistance. After all, don't we want them to hear ours?

I support the people I care about in healthy, loving ways.

ALMOST ALL AFRICAN-AMERICANS have lost their original religion, language, and homeland. Most Native Americans also have lost their land, customs, and language. And after years in this country, descendants of Hispanic and Asian immigrants often forego their native tongue in favor of English.

These are cultural losses that can affect us profoundly. What we lose, we can't pass on to the next generation. Discrimination can cause loss of opportunity and self-esteem. The daily struggles and injustices can make us feel hopeless and lost. But we mustn't give up.

Let's remember the power we do have. Let's remember our mettle and fortitude. If it has been too long since we've felt hope and confidence, we can reach deep inside ourselves to find it. We can ask our loved ones to help us find our way again. We can turn to the Good Lord for peace and direction. With help, we can rediscover our sacred selves.

Grieve your losses but never give up hope. The light within us can be the light at the end of the tunnel.

I pray for strength and illumination to survive my losses and persevere.

Get Centered *May 18*

EVERY PERSON HAS A CENTER THAT includes curiosity, vitality, joy, intelligence, and love; it is our connection to the spiritual force in the universe. However, we may cover up our centers as protection against life's hurts—such as racism, sexism, child abuse, and domestic violence. The only problem with this method of coping is that we feel off balance when we deny our center.

When we are centered, we let go of our defense mechanisms and act out of the place where our highest selves live. We are in touch with our spiritual power, therefore, we feel whole, vital, and serene. When we ignore, deny, or forget the spiritual flow within us, we become listless, afraid, depressed, and even physically ill.

When we are centered, we are effective because we are operating out of the part of ourselves where God exists. When we are centered, our moods don't fluctuate so wildly. We don't have ecstatic highs and devastating lows. We maintain a calm, steady demeanor.

I am centered in truth, reality, and love.

Malcolm X's Birthday *May 19*

MALCOLM X WENT FROM SMALL-time hustler to prisoner to follower of the Nation of Islam to one of this century's outstanding revolutionary leaders. He went from hating himself to hating whites to hating no one. He chose a life of honor and integrity rather than a life of thievery. He taught himself the history he didn't read about in school. He availed himself of spiritual guidance he hadn't found in his church. If Malcolm X had lived, there is no telling where he would have gone because his philosophies were always expanding to fit the new insights he gained.

Let's honor his memory today by committing ourselves to our growth as Malcolm X dedicated himself to his. Just as Malcolm X used imprisonment, we have the same power to use our misfortunes to gain clarity and learn the truth about ourselves. We are more fortunate than he because we have more opportunity to learn. There are more books and classes about our respective cultures than ever before. There is more freedom in this country to explore our own visions than ever before.

Of the many lessons Malcolm X taught, perhaps the most important one is to know ourselves. We can carry on his legacy by evolving ourselves.

I am always evolving into a higher version of myself.

A HELPFUL DEFINITION FOR SUCCESS might be: that which manifests our highest good and the good of those around us. Therefore, people who are living with honesty, decency, and honor are a success. They may not have fancy cars, fur coats, or diamond rings, but they have something much more important: integrity.

Unfortunately, this nation usually defines success in terms of financial gain. Tragically, too many of us have bought into this lie at the price of our health, communities, and ultimately our souls. The sad folks who try to use a BMW as the entrée into a society based on material wealth know this. The spiritless youth who deal in drugs and weapons for a few gold chains and a low-riding car must know at some level they are selling themselves along with the crack.

We are successful when we are true to ourselves and our purpose. We are successful when we reach out to our fellow men and women and give of ourselves. Unless we can look in the mirror and like what we see, we'll never know true victory or true peace.

I live with integrity and my reward is success.

FEAR IS QUIET. IT CREEPS UP ON US AND whispers in our ears: "You're worthless. Don't try. Give up. You'll fail." Over generations we begin to listen. Over more generations we forget that it is fear speaking and begin to think it is ourselves.

But we can let go of fear and find our voices again. All that space taken up by fear becomes free to hold love. Love is the opposite of fear.

When we operate in fear, we drink, take drugs, overeat, and otherwise abuse ourselves. We treat people—even our friends and families—with hatred, selfishness, greed, and dishonesty. *We react.*

When we operate in love, we nurture and care for ourselves. We treat others with kindness, concern, respect, and gentleness. *We act.*

Releasing fear can be painful. For many of us, it's been a long-time companion. We may have to grieve the loss of our sneaky confidant. It is time to walk with a new and better friend—love.

I say good-bye to fear and hello to love.

A TALKING CIRCLE IS A NATIVE AMERIcan custom that enables a group of people to share their experience, strength, and hope. When two or more people join together with honesty and willingness, another force enters the room. The power that is greater than us is actually tangible in the air. The participants can see it in one another's eyes and feel it inside their hearts. The healing energy touches each person and transforms them. What is this power? *Love.*

When we share ourselves with each other, when we give each other our undivided attention, we are declaring our love in the most profound way. I'm not talking about romantic love, though all relationships flourish with attention. I'm talking about the love of our brothers and sisters that we feel when we cut through the superficial differences that keep us apart. Black, brown, red, white, yellow, male, and female can come together and learn from each other. We all bring something valuable to life's experience.

Whether in a talking circle, AA meeting, or prayer group, we can hear the voice of God in others and listen to its wisdom.

I avail myself of the healing power of fellowship.

IT'S NATURAL TO WANT TO LASH OUT AND hurt those who have hurt us, but we cannot right past wrongs by committing similar acts. Having an affair to get back at the spouse who cheated on us does not erase the pain of infidelity. No vengeful act can take away the hurt.

We would benefit more from seeking and accepting apology when it's realistic. However, we cannot make a person change if they don't want to. All we can do is tell our lovers, pals, or colleagues how we feel because of their behavior. Their willingness to make amends is up to them. Usually, if we share a sincere grievance with well-adjusted people, they will welcome the conversation. Mature people are not threatened by confrontation.

We also could put our vengeful energies to better use by pursuing social change for the future, rather than restitution for the past. What's been done has been done. Though we should never forget it, we should let it go. There's too much that needs our attention in the present. Holding grudges only hurts us. Society only can make amends to us by giving us justice today.

I release any desire to punish and replace it with a desire to forgive and amend.

WHEN EUROPEANS ARRIVED ON these shores, they felt superior to the natives who met them. And with every tide of immigration since, there has been a backlash of prejudice. Slaves and immigrants from Oriental and Latin countries were like the ocean: wave after wave hitting the beach, leaving the sand black, brown, and yellow.

The effects of being denied citizenship and civil rights linger and can make us feel less than human, less than worthy. Discrimination leaves a strong stench in the air, which fills our lungs with shame, as if we had done something wrong. As if we were wrong, when the only "damage" we have done is survive.

Let's clear the air. We are not second-class citizens and we shouldn't act like it.

I breathe in the fresh air of truth and know my worth.

ENJOYING OUR SENSUALITY IS NOT ONLY about our sex lives. It's about appreciating our senses, being aware of all that is around us. Our cultures offer many opportunities to rejoice in our senses. We shouldn't take for granted our ability to hear, see, smell, touch, and taste. We should appreciate the smells and tastes of our food, colors of our skin and dress, and sounds of our languages and music.

Here's an exercise to heighten awareness of your senses: Run your hand across a tree and feel the jagged texture of its bark. Inhale the earthy perfume of its leaves. Watch the sunlight stream through its branches. If the tree bears fruit, taste it. Listen to the wind blow through its branches. . . . Can you hear what it is trying to tell you?

Take pleasure in your senses. It will enhance your enjoyment of eating, moving, and living. Oh, and by the way, it's not bad for your sex life either!

I take a juicy bite out of life and thank God for the use of my senses.

Individuality *May 26*

No two people on earth are alike, and it's got to be that way in music or it isn't music. —BILLIE HOLIDAY

LISTEN CAREFULLY TO ONE OF YOUR favorite songs. Every instrument infuses a different sound, a different nuance. Pianos, drums, flutes, guitars, and saxophones all add a distinct tone yet together they blend to create a new sound they couldn't generate alone.

Human beings are like that. Each person contributes a unique melody to the music of life. However, American society encourages us to assimilate and follow the crowd. If we do so, we lose our particular rhythm and get the blues. We need to treasure and protect our one-of-a-kind voices because they strengthen the entire symphony. We also should respect the individuality of our brothers and sisters, for our own songs would be incomplete without their harmony.

I sing my own song loudly and clearly and allow others to do the same. I enjoy the remarkable music that resonates within and around me.

A simple prayer of thanksgiving was an instruction to all living things. A mourning dove sings a thanksgiving song. A...smile was a thanksgiving for life. In the beginning, we knew this prayer because we knew life and we were thankful.

—TSEWAA

WE CAN BE THANKFUL FOR ALL THE blessings in our lives. Grateful for sorrow as well as for joy; for the end of a relationship as well as for the beginning; for illness as well as for health.

Gratitude isn't the first feeling that comes to mind when we are suffering. But misery has much to teach us.

My mother's unsuccessful battle with cancer was the most painful experience of my life. Yet, the experience taught me to enjoy my friends and family while they are with me. And it taught me that I could experience deep pain and survive. I am wiser and stronger for having gone through the experience. And for that I am thankful.

We don't have to wait until we lose someone to feel grateful for what they give us. We don't even have to wait until Thanksgiving Day to count our blessings. Today, we can think of all the things for which we are grateful and say a simple prayer of thanksgiving.

I thank the Great Spirit for all that life has given me—the sweet as well as the bitter.

Family Roles *May 28*

PEOPLE IN DYSFUNCTIONAL FAMILIES are like characters in a twisted theatrical production, thriving on drama and make-believe. "Scapegoat," "Forgotten Child," "Enabler," and "Superachiever" are just some of the roles members can play. Each person's part depends on the others staying in character; for the actors truly believe that if they just listen to their cues and stick to the script, they'll live happily ever after. Of course, this isn't so.

No matter what happened to us as children, we are grown now. The play is over. We can turn the house lights up, let the curtain come down, and end the performance. We can stop pretending to agree if we don't agree. We can stop acting strong if we feel weak. And we can stop faking happiness. We don't have to carry our childhood role into adulthood. The only way to achieve a happy finale is to end the show. Now.

I stop acting and start living in reality.

Mentoring *May 29*

Remember that our cause is one, and that we must help each other, if we would succeed. —FREDERICK DOUGLASS

IT'S IMPORTANT FOR THOSE OF US WHO have made it to the next rung on the ladder to reach back and bring someone along with us. Whatever we have been successful at—careers, surviving an illness, keeping our family together, surmounting a divorce—there are people facing the same issues who could use our help. We can volunteer at a hospice, homeless shelter, or drug and alcohol treatment clinic. We can share our experience, strength, and hope with others.

We also can be mentors for those around us. When we are successful, people observe us looking for clues about how we achieved our goals. Without saying a word to us, they might be inspired by the example we have set. We must realize our catalytic effect on people and be open if people question us about how we have coped.

We also must serve as role models for our children—the children born to us and the children in our communities. A living, breathing success story can do more to invalidate negative stereotypes and raise hopes than any hypothetical case study.

I inspire and encourage those around me with my every action.

HUMAN BEINGS HAVE A STRONG SPIRITual bond with the earth; a connection with the Motherland that bore us. Unfortunately, many of us are separated from our homelands. Africans lost their homeland through forced immigration. The homeland of the Cherokee, Zuni, Apache, and Crow was stolen from them. Recent Mexican, Cuban, Colombian, Chinese, and Vietnamese immigrants said good-bye to their countries to come to America.

No matter how long ago we left our homes, in our ancestral memories we long to recapture what they meant to us. America may have given us much, but those of us who yearn for our culture are finding ways to bring it back to our lives. We can keep our connection to our homelands. Afrocentric attire and Indian ceremonies are just two examples. We don't have to engage in a battle between our "Americanized" selves and our roots. We can honor our American heritage and our original ancestry at the same time.

Home is deep inside my heart; I can return whenever I choose.

Trust *May 31*

LIVING IN A RACIST SOCIETY TEACHES us to be on guard. Because we don't trust "the system" to protect us, we are always vigilantly on the lookout for people who might take advantage of us or discount us. And if we come from a less-than-healthy family, childhood disappointments may have repeated the lesson that we can't trust anybody or anything. We go through life being suspicious and acting tough.

To be happy, we must learn to trust again. We can start by trusting something easy. For some, a Higher Power might be the most trustworthy entity in their lives. For others, trusting God is difficult. They doubt the presence of a loving force when they have experienced so much hatred and pain. If trusting God is peaceful for you, trust more. If trusting God feels impossible right now, trust what you can. Can you put your faith in your children, mate, friends, fate…yourself? You might have to start by trusting small things like that the bus will arrive on time or your paycheck will be in the mailbox when it is due.

Practice faith little by little. Pray. Invoke the spirit of your ancestors and ask them to help you trust as they trusted.

I am willing to trust.

It's OK to Make Mistakes *June 1*

IT'S OK TO MAKE MISTAKES. IF WE haven't learned that lesson yet, it's time we teach it to ourselves. True, mistakes can cause problems and we should stay aware to minimize errors. However, making mistakes also can help *solve* problems. Some of the greatest inventions, penicillin for example, were discovered by mistake.

None of us is perfect; we *will* make mistakes so we may as well accept that knowledge. No matter how careful we are, sooner or later we'll break a glass, bounce a check, miss a deadline, or forget an appointment.

Fear of making mistakes keeps us stuck in our comfort zones. Today, we can give ourselves permission to make mistakes. If we know that it's OK to make mistakes, we feel free to experiment. With experimentation comes learning and growth.

I accept myself even when I mess up, and I learn from my mistakes.

Express Your Pain *June 2*

THERE ARE MANY WAYS TO EXPRESS our pain. We can join a support group, work with a therapist, go to confession, or share with a friend. We can scream, cry, rage, and yell. Sometimes it's hard for us to let our emotions out, but it might help to try more inventive ways to share our feelings. Art is an age-old means of self-expression that we can use. We can paint, draw, or write about what has hurt us. No matter what method we choose, the important thing is to release the pain so we can heal our wounds.

Visualize your pain as a kite wrapped around your arm; make it any color you want. Imagine that you are out in wide open spaces, alone or with friends, as you prefer. Tell the pain (the kite) whatever you want. Then let it go and watch it disappear above the clouds.

No matter how devastating, we can express our pain. And when we do, we will heal.

I name my pain and begin to heal.

Denial *June 3*

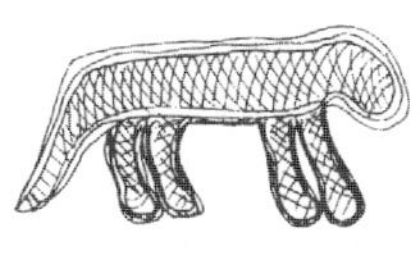

USUALLY WHEN PEOPLE SAY SOMEone is in denial, they mean it in a negative way. However, denial serves an important purpose. It acts as a protective shield to allow us to come to terms with our distress when we are ready. It is nature's safety belt that braces us for the shock of an explosive impact.

Typically the first thing we feel when we experience a traumatic event is shock. Disbelief might cause us to pretend the event didn't happen. Children, especially, deny abuses they suffer at the hands of parents or other trusted parties. The shock wears off when we are physically, mentally, emotionally, and spiritually equipped to handle the awareness.

In order to progress, we must work through our denial. While the brutal truth may be necessary for some to let go of denial, we would do better by accepting the truth in manageable doses. When we feel ready, we can find a safe person and place to let go and feel the powerful emotions that come when we move beyond denial.

Give yourself gentle nudges to move beyond denial, but forgive yourself if you aren't ready to change yet. It will happen when you are ready.

With my Higher Power's love I can release denial and face my pain.

Don't Settle — *June 4*

What I have seen is that, too often, our people give in to the expectations that the dominant society has placed on us and settle for much less than dignity and self-respect should allow. —JOHN DAVID MENDOZA BRODEUR

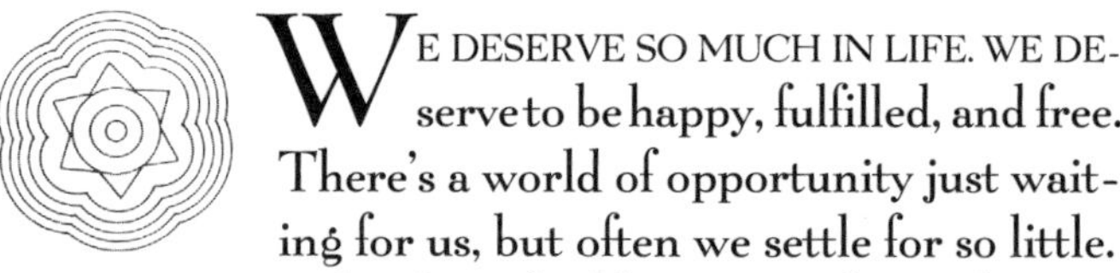

WE DESERVE SO MUCH IN LIFE. WE DEserve to be happy, fulfilled, and free. There's a world of opportunity just waiting for us, but often we settle for so little.

We accept loveless, faithless, or violent relationships when we could know true caring from others. We tolerate dead-end jobs when we could have satisfying, rewarding careers. We settle for lives of desperation when we could know peace and serenity.

Our lives are what we have allowed. Today, let's make a commitment to achieve all that we can in life. We deserve all the good that life has to offer. Don't settle for anything less.

I allow joy, serenity, health, and prosperity into my life because I know I deserve them.

Staying in the Now *June 5*

MOST PEOPLE ARE PRONE TO SPENDing time in yesterday or tomorrow and not really appreciating today. We reminisce about the past and long for "the good old days" of high school or when our children were little or when our relationship was new. Or we agonize or dream about the future wondering if this, that, or the other will happen.

Planning and setting goals are healthy. Enjoying pleasant memories also can be good for us. But the only time we have is this moment. Yesterday is gone and tomorrow may not come. As you are reading these words, where is your mind? Are you focused on this thought?

Our elders knew the importance of today. We can take a page out of their book and savor the time we have now. Time, like money, can be spent. However, there is no bank we can withdraw time from when we need it. There's no credit card we can use to buy more time. We only get a finite amount, and we'll never know how much. Today is the only dollar in your pocket. Spend it wisely.

I consciously live each moment as if it is the only one I have…because it is.

Legacy for Our Children *June 6*

PARENTS, PEERS, SIBLINGS, TEACHERS, media figures, sports heros, and movie stars influence a child's self-image. The lucky kids are the kids that get to filter through all they see and hear and decide for themselves who they are.

Children develop their own identities very early in life. Parents often talk about babies having personalities, complete with likes and dislikes. Unfortunately, many adults don't know how to let the child's personality continue to develop.

We can give guidance and set standards for appropriate behavior. We can teach our children what is acceptable and what is not, but we can't make them be who we want them to be. Let's stop expecting children to be little carbon copies of ourselves. We can benefit from respecting our children more and listening to what they have to say. They have much to teach us.

The greatest gift we can give our children is permission to be themselves. Whatever your relation to a child—parent, godmother, uncle, or grandmother—you can be a role model and teach self-respect and integrity.

I instruct the children I know in the art of being true to themselves by demonstrating that I am true to myself.

Journaling — *June 7*

A JOURNAL CAN BE A WONDERFUL confidant: it never gives advice, always has time to listen, affirms our growth, and accepts us exactly as we are. The pages of a journal are filled with opportunity for enlightenment, healing, and maturity.

When we fill the pages with our hopes and dreams, we set in motion our ability to make them real. When we record our fears and worries, we release ourselves from their stranglehold on us and free ourselves to love. Once we have worked through our doubts, we can remind ourselves of how we've successfully faced similar challenges. Ah, and when we write of love! There is no finer literature. If we are inspired to pen thoughts of our beloved, we can enjoy them alone or share them with our sweethearts.

A journal is a tool we use to help us connect with our thoughts and feelings. When we put issues down on paper, the fog lifts and the way becomes clear. Write today about what moves you. Your confidant is waiting to listen.

I gather my thoughts like a bouquet of flowers and plant them in the pages of my journal. Like the flowers, I become grounded.

Risky Business — *June 8*

Risks are perceived illusions that I find limiting to the imagination. The imagination will blossom without any self-induced boundaries.
—ROBERT BOGGESS

I'M NOT TALKING ABOUT BUNGEE JUMPING, skydiving, drag racing, sleeping with strangers, or having unprotected sex "just this once." Those are risks it just doesn't pay to take.

Today's reading refers to emotional and mental decisions that often feel like risks. If we are afraid to trust others we can create a "banking" system to judge if a person is trustworthy. If they have deposited many trustworthy acts, then it's probably safe to trust them. However, if they've lied and acted unreliably, their account is empty. We would be wise to disbelieve what they tell us. This process gives us information to make a calculated risk.

We can balance the pros and cons in all such ventures—forgiving an infidelity, taking a new job, moving to another city, or starting a business. If the benefits outweigh the drawbacks, we can go ahead and take the gamble.

I inventory what threatens me about living. If there are "risky" endeavors that would enhance my growth, I pray for the courage to take them.

Surrender *June 9*

WE ARE SCRAPPERS. TO BE BLACK, Hispanic, Asian, or American Indian in this country is to know battle. We've had to fight for liberty, citizenship, and civil rights. Because the struggle continues, we may not know when to stop fighting. We may keep attacking a problem that can't be conquered by aggression; it's like banging our heads against a wall. Sometimes the best offense is surrender.

I'm not suggesting we resign ourselves to the difficulties in our lives. I'm simply suggesting that we may need to stop and review if our actions are helping or hurting our cause. Sometimes if we stop, we'll discover there is a better way.

We can surrender ourselves to our Higher Power. We can let God take up our cause and help us with our conflicts. We do not have to go it alone.

In fact, sometimes the best way to approach a problem is to stop fighting it.

I let go and let God.

Self-Worth — *June 10*

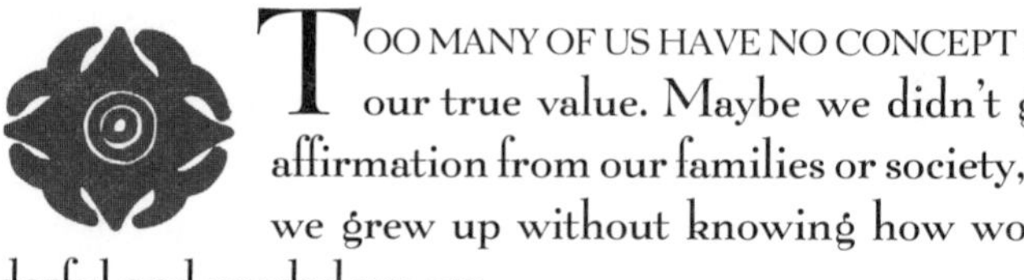

TOO MANY OF US HAVE NO CONCEPT OF our true value. Maybe we didn't get affirmation from our families or society, so we grew up without knowing how wonderful and needed we are.

Every person has a purpose to fulfill, a reason they are here. We are all just one part of the universal puzzle. The problems that face our neighborhoods, this country, and the world can be conquered if each one of us does our part. Therefore, each individual has value. When we know our purpose, we know our worth.

We can build our sense of self by focusing on our positive attributes, complimenting ourselves, and giving ourselves praise. Beating up on ourselves only leads to more shame and more negativity. Low self-esteem is an insatiable dragon; when we feed it, it only gets hungrier. Nourish self-worth; feed yourself with kindness, knowledge, patience, and love.

We are all necessary to God's plan. I play my part with complete knowledge of how valuable I am.

The Closet *June 11*

WE DON'T HAVE TO BE GAY TO LIVE IN "the closet." Due to the harsh treatment of our ancestors and the injustices we see today, we may have developed a false self—a cover to protect us. However, the persona we create as protection may hurt us more in the long run.

The false self has no feelings, no thoughts. It keeps its mouth shut and stays out of the way. Therefore, we may become disconnected from our true self. We do ourselves no favor by putting on an act. The pretense only causes pain because the person deep inside wants to be known. By denying ourselves the right to be who we are—for whatever reason—we subjugate ourselves. There is no worse injury than the self-inflicted wound.

Our real selves are lurking just beneath the surface and longing for daylight. We deserve to explore our dreams and desires and there's no room to stretch ourselves in a closet. Gay or straight, we can open the doors and allow ourselves to breathe the fresh air of truth and dignity.

I shake the mothballs off of my true self. I give myself light and air because, like every living thing, I deserve it.

Take Care of Yourself *June 12*

THIS MIND, BODY, AND SPIRIT ARE THE only ones you'll have. Take care of them! People of color typically age well, but with a little extra dedication we can make sure we enter old age in sound health.

Here are suggestions for taking care of yourself:

1. Eat nutritiously. A suggestion is to eat more fiber, fruits, and vegetables and limit fats, sugars, and red meat.
2. Be more active. Dance, run, and play more. It will help your bodies and it will lift your spirits.
3. Laugh a lot. Find the joy in life. A good joke a day may help keep the doctor away.
4. Pray a lot. Turn to the universal force for wisdom and direction. Let your Higher Power guide you in all your affairs.
5. Balance your time. Find time for yourself to be alone. But also spend time with loved ones.

We need balance to maintain emotional, mental, physical, and spiritual well-being. One of the best things we can do for the people we love is to make sure we're around to share their lives.

I take good care of myself. I am worthy of my own time and attention.

PEOPLE OF COLOR HAVE HAD TO DEvelop the strength of John Henry in order to cope with the travesties and indignities to which we are often subjected. We can use that strength to teach our children that crime and drugs are not a part of our culture. Dealers, gang bangers, and cokeheads are symptoms of oppression, not culture. We can use that strength to clean up our streets and teach our brothers and sisters who have gone astray that there is a better way.

We can use that strength to handle personal decisions about life, work, and relationships. If the life we have isn't what we want, we're going to have to change and that takes courage.

We can build ourselves up physically, so our bodies can better handle the stresses of life. Walking, swimming, riding our bikes, or dancing will strengthen our lungs and hearts, and lifting weights will strengthen our muscles. We also can fortify ourselves mentally, emotionally, and spiritually. With attention and care, we can be as strong as Cuban coffee.

The world needs me to be strong, so I nurture my inherent strength.

Persistence *June 14*

When you begin a great work, you can't expect to finish it all at once; therefore do you and your brothers press on, and let nothing discourage you till you have entirely finished what you have begun. —TEEDYUSCUNG

WRITING A BOOK, EARNING A DEgree, losing weight, developing a relationship all take time. Sometimes in the middle of working toward a goal, we lose our motivation. We tell ourselves we're bored or tired or that we just can't do it. But what may really be going on is that we're afraid.

It's OK to feel afraid—that's human. And it's good for us to know that's how we're feeling. Then we can do something about it. We may need a rest. It's OK to take time out to rejuvenate ourselves before we move forward. We also can seek support and encouragement from friends, family, and our Higher Power. We can turn to the universal love and wisdom that is in our hearts and let it nourish us.

Then, when we are ready, we can *gently* press on. That means we break down tasks into simple, manageable activities and take them one step at a time. Before you know it, you'll have reached your goal.

When I feel overwhelmed, I allow myself to take a deep breath and relax. Then I move forward.

Limits *June 15*

FOR THE MOST PART, WE ARE GOOD, decent, responsible people, but we're never perfect. We will always make mistakes. There is no shame in being flawed.

Only God is perfect. Only God is limitless. Humans, in our earthly form, are finite. We will live in this plane of existence for only a certain number of years and then life as we know it will cease. We may be reborn in some way, but the person we are now will be no more. Being armed with the knowledge of our limitations can allow us to act more wisely and not waste the precious resources we have.

Let's not waste time. Why take today's sunshine for granted when it might rain tomorrow? Let's not waste the wisdom our elders have passed on to us. We are finite beings.

I humbly accept my limits.

Blessing Instead of Curse *June 16*

THOSE OF US WHO HAVE SUFfered through tough experiences (rough childhood, addiction, divorce) at first may see only the horror, only the pain. With healing, though, we gain perspective. We realize that what we initially perceived as a curse may have been a blessing.

This isn't to say that we are happy about our hardship, but that we begin to understand that, in addition to the suffering, we gained insights and strengths that we wouldn't have obtained otherwise. Some people who survived cancer or who are living with AIDS are able to express gratitude for what their illness has taught them. Perhaps they had to get sick to learn to be assertive. Or they perceived their ailment as a wake-up call to take better care of themselves. Recovering alcoholics and addicts also often say they are thankful for their disease because it brought them to deeper understandings of spirituality and fellowship.

What doesn't kill us only makes us stronger. Today, let's make a decision to see the advantages instead of the drawbacks.

I give thanks for the events in my life that taught me to survive and made me strong.

Be Open-Minded *June 17*

SOMETIMES WE JUMP TO CONCLUSIONS. We "can tell" the lady in the grocery store is being mean because she's a racist. We "just know" our lover hasn't called because he or she is having an affair. Or our supervisor "must be" picking on us out of spite. Unless we have some evidence to confirm these ideas, they are just assumptions.

Did the check-out clerk make a racist remark? Perhaps she's just in a hurry or having a bad day. Maybe our lover hasn't called because he or she needs some time alone. Does our manager treat the other employees the same, or are we being singled out?

We need to listen to our intuition on such matters; however, sometimes our inner feelings bias our understanding of what happens around us. Let's keep an open mind about what drives another person's behavior until we have proof.

Assumptions lead to miscommunication, hurt feelings, and bad judgment. It's the same lack of open-mindedness that causes a bigot to stereotype us based on our skin color, language, or clothing. Rather than make rash decisions, let's keep an open mind.

I seek the truth and keep an open mind.

THE HUMAN SPIRIT IS INVINCIBLE, UNdestroyable. Racism, sexism, and all the other affronts we must face battle the human spirit, but they will not win. Our spirits are linked with the universal flow of life. No matter how tired, defeated, and embittered we may feel, our spirits still will soar if we let them.

Our spirits live on in the face of boredom, indecision, and frustration. Our spirits live on in the face of torment, horror, and injustice. Even after we die, our hearts stop beating and our lungs stop expelling air, but our spirits live on. No matter what problems we are facing today, let's keep close to our hearts the knowledge that we will overcome, we will prevail.

I am spirit-filled and, with my Higher Power's love and guidance, I can handle anything that comes my way.

JUNETEENTH COMMEMORATES THE day in 1865 when slaves in Texas finally were freed by the Emancipation Proclamation. African-Americans around the country celebrate with dances, picnics, festivals, and speeches.

Even if we don't celebrate today as a holiday, we have much to cheer about. It's a beautiful day at the beginning of summer. Today would be a good day to enjoy the sunshine, greenery, warmth, and the delicious foods that taste best this time of year. Perhaps for the first time this year, we can take a dip in the ocean, lake, or neighborhood swimming pool. We can walk barefoot and feel the warm earth or wet sand between our toes. Or we can listen to a concert in the park, host a barbecue, or throw a block party.

We can honor the sweet taste of liberty savored by the last slaves in the United States by appreciating our freedom to enjoy this day. We are free. We can celebrate however we choose. Isn't that wonderful?

I celebrate my liberty today and every day.

Pride June 20

I believe in pride of race and lineage and self; in pride of self so deep as to scorn injustice to other selves. —W. E. B. DUBOIS

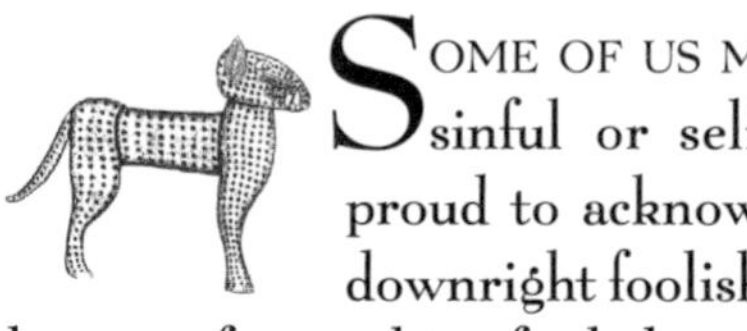

SOME OF US MAY FEEL THAT PRIDE IS sinful or selfish. Indeed, being too proud to acknowledge our limitations is downright foolish. That type of arrogance keeps us from asking for help and from becoming all that we can. But there is another kind of pride that is based on dignity and self-esteem; on always doing our best. This is the pride we celebrate today.

We demonstrate our pride by our actions. Show yourself and the world you are proud by treating yourself and others with respect. Look at your dress, language, and manners, and change whatever doesn't show pride of self. Let's be proud of our talents, characteristics, achievements. If you have strong arms or pretty legs, show them off. If you have recently received a degree or a promotion, tell somebody. We can savor our accomplishments without putting others down.

Teach pride. Encourage those around us to be proud of themselves. If your son or daughter got an A in school, call the aunties and tell them. Take your mate to dinner to acknowledge his or her success. Tell the people you love you are proud of them.

I show my pride today.

THERE IS REALITY AND OUR PERCEPTION of reality. Reality: It rained one hundred days last year. Perception: We thought it rained a lot. Perhaps. But if we look at an almanac, maybe we'll find that one hundred days of rain is the average for annual precipitation. We need to verify our perceptions before we act on them.

Our intuition is powerful and should neither be ignored nor denied. We think our spouse is being unfaithful or a co-worker is trying to sabotage us. Before we make accusations, let's sit down and review the facts to make sure our feelings aren't coloring reality. If there is evidence that something is amiss, then we can act.

Reviewing our perceptions will help us get in touch with our feelings. Sometimes internalized shame will make us think no one could possibly love us so we look for evidence to prove that. When in reality, everybody else knows we are lovable. If we are insecure, that will color everything we see.

Sometimes our intuition is on target. We don't need "proof"; our inner voice is talking to us loudly and clearly. Take time to get to know yourself so you know whether your perceptions are being shaped by the wise part of you or by the insecure part.

My perceptions are based on reality.

OPPRESSION TEACHES US THAT SOMEthing is wrong with us: Our skin is the wrong shade. Our tresses don't flow the right way. Our eyes are the wrong shape. And we just don't talk right. Oppression leaves a legacy of shame.

We must oppose shaming thoughts, feelings, and words. We must stop believing lies about our worth. Each one of us has so much to offer this world. Each one of us is a child of God. Completely unique, yet like every other human being, brimming with goodness.

Today, let's take action and defeat shame. Let's create a shame-free zone for ourselves in which we will not criticize nor allow others to criticize us. Within our zone we will allow only loving thoughts, kind deeds, and supportive expressions. We can invite others into our shame-free zone if they are willing to abide by the no-criticism rule. A shame-free zone would be healing for us all.

I do not blame, shame, or criticize. I allow only gentleness, compassion, and considerateness into my world.

THE CYCLES OF LIFE, THE CYCLES OF nature, the connection between the tides and the moon, the cycle of the planets that revolve around the sun are all understood by our people. Like the other cycles in life, there is a cycle of healing. And in order to heal, we must allow ourselves to go through this cycle. It won't be easy and it won't be fun but it will be good for us.

Healing begins with acknowledgment—recognizing the presence of a wound. We don't like to admit our pain because it hurts. But we are just fooling ourselves by thinking if we don't acknowledge the pain, it will go away.

The cycle then moves into feeling anger, grief, betrayal, shame, and rage. We can accept, feel deeply, and then let go. We don't have to hold on forever. There is an ebb and flow to emotions just as there is to the tides.

Allow yourself to move through the cycle of healing at whatever pace your soul needs to move.

I move through the cycle of healing like the stars travel across the sky.

Direction *June 24*

THERE ARE MANY TWISTS AND TURNS along the road of life. During those moments when we are in doubt about which direction to follow, we can ask God to show us the way. The Creator Spirit will always direct us to the right places at the right times. Higher guidance also comes from other people. We should listen to those that we have selected to share our journeys with. They are here to share God's messages. Our friends and relatives, and even our enemies, can be the answer to our prayers.

My Grandfather, the Great Spirit, steers me in the right direction.

Satori — *June 25*

光

SATORI IS A JAPANESE WORD USED BY Zen Buddhists to describe the feeling of enlightenment or insight: an epiphany. Buddhists seek satori through meditation.

In addition to meditation, we can use prayer and reading to shed light on our problems. No matter which method we choose, the important issue is that we look for solutions. It is crucial that we choose to walk out of the darkness of ignorance and into the light of knowledge. Wisdom and direction come to those who seek them.

My Higher Power illuminates my path and brightens my heart.

Collective Responsibility *June 26*

CONTRARY TO WHAT THE MEDIA might tell us, people of color value family, education, and collective responsibility. However, some of us aren't acting on those beliefs because of the legacy of oppression. Some of us have bought into the stereotypes and lies about ourselves and started acting on the "every man for himself" mentality.

Early men and women came together to live in groups because they knew they could not survive alone. Our ancestors carried on this tradition and created villages, pueblos, and towns to benefit each other. We must do the same for our communities today.

We can't control the kids who would rather shoot up or shoot each other than shoot hoops. We can't control the father who deserts his children nor the mother that ignores them. However, we can control our actions. We can live as an example of mature men and women. We can select one issue and volunteer our time or money to improve it. There are many problems in our community that no one of us can fix, but together we can find solutions. No problem is bigger than the power of people who come together in love, faith, and hope. We may not be our brother's keeper, but we can be his friend.

I share my wisdom with my brothers and sisters.

MODERN LIFE CAN MAKE IT HARD TO live with honor. Every day we meet opportunities that ask us to compromise our principles. We may say to ourselves: "Just this one time, I'll be dishonest" or "What they don't know won't hurt them" or "That's what you have to do to get ahead."

Not true. We do not have to forget our values to succeed in life. We do not have to prostitute ourselves to make a buck. No financial or material gain is worth jeopardizing our principles—no matter what this "nice-guys-finish-last" society tells us.

It all depends on the standards we set for ourselves. If we define the finish line—the goal of our lives—as being peaceful, self-actualizing, loving people, then nice guys and gals finish first. It is when we honor our values that we are most richly rewarded.

We are meant to live with integrity, doing what we know to be right and true for us. It's what God wants for us, and it's what we want for ourselves.

I treat myself with dignity and respect and live with integrity.

Oppression Not Culture *June 28*

AT BEST, SOCIETY CONDESCENDingly teaches that our customs and ceremonies are colorful, antiquated rituals. At worst, we learn that negative behavior—such as sexism, laziness, theft, and addiction—is born out of our culture.

However, much of the inappropriate behavior attributed to our culture is actually the result of oppression. When people are mistreated, devalued, and disrespected, they develop patterns of behavior to cope. If they don't heal from the abuse, the coping skills become ingrained patterns.

We act out these patterns where it is safe—against ourselves and others like us. Think of the child who is beaten by his parents and then bullies other kids. Society observes fetal alcohol syndrome, crack babies, "black-on-black" crime, and riots that destroy our own neighborhoods and mistakes them for culture.

This is not to condone or excuse violent and uncouth actions, but rather to explain where they come from. Culture does not encourage negative behavior... oppression does.

I am aware of how oppression has affected me and other people of color, and I separate the results of oppression from my culture.

Juggling — *June 29*

I'm doing the best I can, I'm going to do the best I can, and that's all any one human being can do, isn't it?

—THEA VIDALE

WE HAVE A VARIETY OF RESPONSIBILITIES—work, play, school, family, friends, and so on. Sometimes we may feel like jugglers with too many balls in the air. People of color have learned to handle many things at once, and many of us are good at it. However, we don't have to do everything at once.

Life is not a performance. We don't have to try to "wow" an audience by juggling more and more balls. If we feel overwhelmed, we can do ourselves a favor by allowing ourselves to limit the activities we participate in. We can choose which balls we want to juggle. The trick is neither to overestimate nor to underestimate how many we can handle. We learn to judge our capabilities through trial and error. With practice, we'll know how much we can take on and still maintain our peace of mind.

All I can do is all I can do, and that is good enough.

Pamper Day *June 30*

INSTEAD OF USING THIS PAMPER DAY TO live it up, let's use it to quiet down. Take an entire day (or as much time as possible) and sit quietly; partake of focused relaxation. Meditate. Listen to soothing music. Read. Reflect. Write in a journal. Spend the day in solitude and contemplation.

We often spend so much time focusing on others that we forget who we are. We can tell in a heartbeat what the children want, what our mate needs, what our boss requires. But what do we want and need? Let's use today to get to know ourselves again. Let's use today to renew our commitment to our purpose.

We may have hectic schedules and many demands for our time, but we will benefit from preserving a little time for ourselves. We actually save time in the long run, because when we are calm and centered, we are much more effective people. If we can't devote an entire day to meditation, surely we can find fifteen minutes. Whether an hour or a day, we all need time to rest our minds and spirits. Taking time out allows us to harness our energy and focus it in the appropriate direction. After reflecting, we can go back to our daily lives rejuvenated and ready.

The time I take to ensure my mental health and spiritual well-being pays off.

Service *July 1*

It's very easy to be a servant, but very difficult to be of service. When you are of service, you're there whether you like it or not, whether it's Sunday, Monday or a holiday. You're there whenever you are needed. — CÉSAR CHÁVEZ

WE ALL HAVE A SERVICE WE CAN PROvide to our community. However, we'll become burned out if we try to be of service to everyone all the time. We can define our community and then make it a priority to be of service to them. It can mean our families, our employer, our neighborhood, our city, and so on. By defining our community, we make our actions more focused and more effective.

In addition to deciding to whom we will be of service, we also need to determine how we will assist them. What talents, knowledge, tools, or crafts do we have to share? If we're good with children, we can volunteer to take neighborhood kids to a museum or library once a month. If we're good writers, we can offer to create a community newsletter. Maybe we're good listeners, bakers, or mechanics. Or maybe we're physically strong. All these abilities are gifts we can give to others. When we give to our community, we give to ourselves.

I put my skills to use assisting my defined community.

Delayed Gratification *July 2*

AMERICAN SOCIETY HAS BECOME addicted to immediate gratification. We complain if our dinner doesn't arrive over the counter in two minutes or less. Instant coffee, instant breakfast...instant success? Most often, it doesn't work like that.

Achieving goals is more like baking bread. Bread must be kneaded, set aside, and given time to rise. Good bread doesn't happen in an instant and neither does success.

We can wean ourselves from the irrational desire to be perfect overnight. We'll never be perfect, but we will mature with experience. With patience and kindness, we can give ourselves the same care and attention fresh-baked bread takes. We can give ourselves a break! We can ease up on our expectations of ourselves. We don't have to stop trying to achieve. We don't have to give up our hopes and desires. We acknowledge that it takes time to accomplish all that we want to do. We put in the time now, knowing the rewards will come later.

I am patient and gentle with myself as I work toward my goals.

Boycott Negativity *July 3*

AS SURELY AS FIGHTERS FOR CIVIL rights boycotted the Birmingham, Alabama, bus system, we must boycott negativity. We don't have to participate in any activity or event that causes negative thoughts or feelings.

Kindness often leads us to try and motivate the negative people we know. Perhaps friends need a push to aspire, hope, and try. However, if we find ourselves cheering them on to no avail, we can stop. Some people in our lives will never grow up or take the leap of faith that maturity requires. If so, we can still love them and protect ourselves from their negative energy. Boycott people who are boring, whining, uninspired, slothful, unwilling, and fearful. Refuse to have dealings with such people because they only bring us down with them.

I don't entertain negative thoughts or negative people. Confidence and faith get me through life.

Independence Day *July 4*

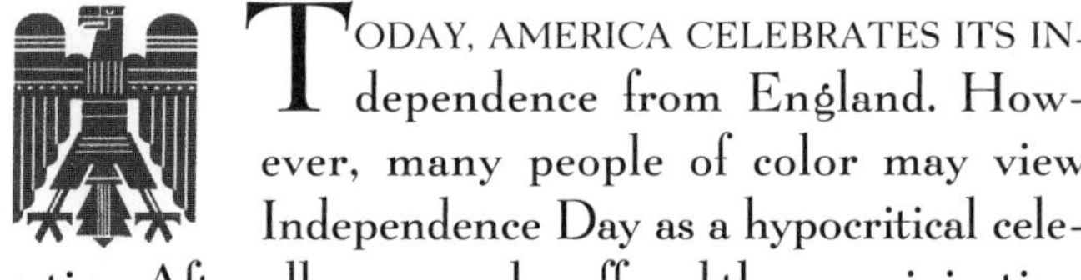

TODAY, AMERICA CELEBRATES ITS INdependence from England. However, many people of color may view Independence Day as a hypocritical celebration. After all, our people suffered the same injustices that this country claimed to be against and other uglier indignities, without receiving independence for centuries. Some of us, who recently escaped a country that limited personal freedoms, may view today with hope for achieving the American dream.

Whatever our feelings about the Fourth of July, we can celebrate our personal independence. If our minds are free of self-defeating thoughts, we are free. If we refuse to treat ourselves like second-class citizens, we are free.

Let Independence Day stand for independence of the mind, heart, and spirit. Let the fireworks and barbecues commemorate our regard for ourselves and our people. We are free and we can celebrate.

Today marks the independence of my soul.

Anger — *July 5*

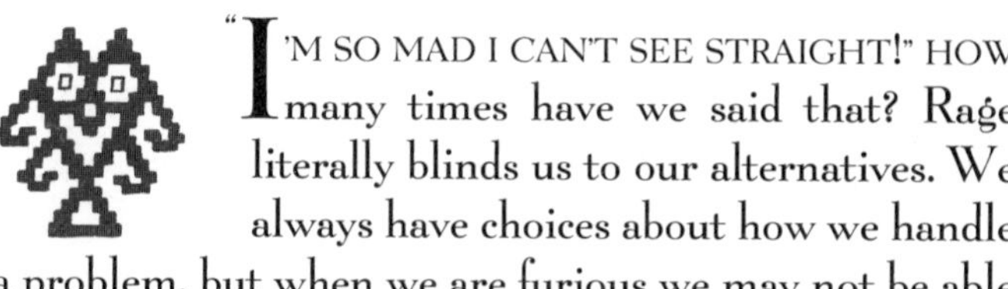

"I'M SO MAD I CAN'T SEE STRAIGHT!" HOW many times have we said that? Rage literally blinds us to our alternatives. We always have choices about how we handle a problem, but when we are furious we may not be able to see them.

It would be helpful for us to buy ourselves some time before we respond to an infuriating situation. Take some deep breaths. Count to ten. Walk around the block. After we cool down, we'll be better able to choose an appropriate course of action.

We probably won't always be able to manage our anger in the most appropriate way, and that's OK. There will be days when we don't want to be appropriate, good, or well-behaved. Maybe we just want to act out. We still can accept ourselves. We're human and we won't always be able to control anger, any more than we can control a spontaneous burst of tears or giggles.

However, we can try to give ourselves time for our vision to clear before we respond to angry feelings.

I wait until I can "see straight" to act on my anger.

Confusion *July 6*

WHEN WE AREN'T CENTERED, WE give ourselves conflicting messages and opposing goals. When we aren't centered, we have no clear priorities, no clear understanding of what is best for us. There is no harmony, only confusion, disorder, and turmoil.

One of the popular sayings from Twelve-Step groups is "Keep it simple." We simplify our lives by focusing on one thing at a time. We simplify our lives by being honest, therefore we don't have to keep track of lies. We simplify our lives by developing clearly defined priorities; if an endeavor doesn't help us meet a top goal, we don't do it.

Modern life is perplexing enough. Don't contribute to your own confusion. Clear your mind of old debris. Rid your life of unsatisfying activities and save your energy for the projects that are meaningful to you.

As some of the great spiritual leaders have said: Simplify, simplify, simplify.

I keep my mind clear and my life simple.

The Shadow *July 7*

THE SHADOW IS THE DEEPEST, DARKEST of the psyche where we put everything about ourselves we dislike, mistrust, or fear. The shadow houses our animal nature—the wild, immoral, passionate, and aggressive parts of ourselves—which the dominant society tells us is evil or wicked. But, if we are like our ancestors, we know the strength of the shadow. We know it can be a wellspring of energy and spontaneity.

There is no need to deny our "dark side," for it has much to offer us. When we try to cut ourselves off from it, we lose the power for expansion and creation it gives us. Often, when we drive the undesirable parts of ourselves into the darkness, we also hide our gifts. We must own the selfish, jealous parts of ourselves without letting them rule our lives. We must make peace with our shadows.

Exploring my shadow nature is like hunting for buried treasure. I find a wealth of power hidden there.

Accepting Emotions *July 8*

FEELINGS ARE NOT BAD, SHAMEFUL, stupid, or crazy. Feelings just are. Happiness is no better than sadness. Joy is no better than anger. Of course, some feelings are more enjoyable than others, but they all serve a purpose. We wouldn't choose an arm and cut off a leg. Why be selective about which feelings we acknowledge?

Feelings are our emotional barometers. They tell us how we're doing and what we need to work on. If we don't use our emotional energy, we run the risk of becoming blocked and dry. Don't be afraid to feel. Emotions are part of a healthy, balanced life.

I accept all my emotions.

A medicine man says prayers. If you believe in him, you can gain strength from his strength. I guess it's a form of psychotherapy. —DR. CONSTANCE PINKERMAN

WHETHER WE HAVE SPECIFIC ISSUES we want to work through, or want to reach a deeper understanding of ourselves, therapy can help. Traditional psychotherapy, nonconventional therapy methods, and self-help groups are means of making psychological breakthroughs. They are tools that we can use to help us be healthy, fulfilled people.

There are also other methods for mending the body, mind, and heart. We can look at anything healing as therapy: song, prayer, chanting, meditation, laughter, massage, dance, sleep, hot baths, long walks, and making love, to name only a few. Many religions and cultures chant to uplift themselves and commune with a higher order. Similar to prayer and meditation, chanting helps clear the mind and focus consciousness. We can use whatever soothes and supports us to face issues head on.

These activities only have therapeutic value when we use them honestly. They lose their power to heal when we use them to avoid our problems.

I serve as my own curandero *(healer) by taking care of my mental, emotion, physical, and spiritual needs.*

Self-Honesty *July 10*

HOW OFTEN WE TRY TO FOOL OURselves! How often we try to convince ourselves of something that we simply do not believe. We deny evidence of a philandering spouse, a troubled child, a dead-end job. Perhaps we lie to ourselves thinking the pain of truth will be worse than the pain of knowing. This isn't so.

Deep inside we already know the truth. And the inner turmoil that comes with trying to deny our knowledge causes emotional, mental, spiritual, and physical pain. More than anything else, we need to be honest with ourselves. We can't expect others to treat us with respect if we don't respect ourselves enough to face the truth. Before anything positive and beneficial can happen in our lives, we need to acknowledge the truth.

We don't have to handle painful knowledge alone. We can turn to the Great Spirit or a loving friend for strength. With truth comes peace of mind, and we deserve serenity.

I respect myself enough to be honest with myself and others.

THE PHRASE "DO THE RIGHT THING" became popular with Spike Lee's movie of the same name. In this time of shifting mores it gets harder to know what the right thing is.

If we are faced with a situation we don't know how to handle, we can turn to the Creator Spirit for guidance and wisdom. We can ask God to help us do what is best for ourselves and everyone concerned. We can simplify the matter by listening to our inner wisdom. Sometimes it may be painful or scary to do the right thing. We may have to make big changes and great sacrifices. But the integrity, dignity, and self-respect that result from ethical, moral behavior are well worth the challenge.

With love in our hearts and God on our side, we can always do the right thing.

I always know what is right for me.

Patience *July 12*

THOSE OF US WHO HAVE HAD TO WAIT generations for equality may not feel like patience is virtuous. It may feel painful to keep waiting for the respect and esteem we deserve. However, being patient doesn't mean being passive. We can think of the way civil-rights workers of the 1960s methodically attacked injustices. These people were far from compliant; they stood firm in their beliefs despite antagonism, conflict, or challenge.

Like them, we can take action to better our situations. We can ask God for what we want, but we also can be patient with the process and ourselves. What we want will come to us when the time is right. There is a universal plan that our lives are part of; when things fit into the plan, we'll have them.

We can think of patience as active waiting: doing all that is within our power and then accepting the divine timing that is meant for us.

I am on a divine schedule. Everything happens when it is supposed to.

Hitting Bottom *July 13*

I'm sick and tired of being sick and tired.

—FANNIE LOU HAMER

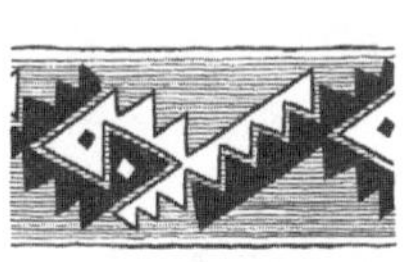

A PERVERSE QUIRK OF HUMAN nature is that sometimes we have to let things get really bad before we admit there is a problem. In recovery groups, they call this progression into despair or disaster "hitting bottom": the person goes as low as he or she can and then he or she is ready to make a change.

People have different "bottoms." Some people get sober after a year or two of heavy drinking. Some don't seek help until they've lost their jobs, spouses, and homes. And others suffer for years and never get help. Hitting bottom doesn't just apply to alcoholism or substance abuse. We may tolerate abusive relationships until we are almost killed, and then we decide to leave. We may work in menial jobs for years before we acknowledge our dissatisfaction and pursue the education and training needed for advancement.

When we hit bottom, we open ourselves to help from friends and God. Allow any problems you face today to serve as a "bottom." Love yourself enough to put an end to misfortune now, before the pain gets worse.

I lovingly face my problems and get the help I need.

Rhythm *July 14*

RHYTHM IS A POWERFUL FORCE within our lives. The beat of the drums echoes in our deepest memories. The meter of poetry. The downbeat in music. Movement of dance speaks to our soul. We move with the cosmic rhythm of the life force.

There is a rhythm and flow to life; sometimes we're up and sometimes we're down. We can help ourselves if we stay tuned to our inner rhythms. We can learn in which part of the day we perform better. Are you a morning or night person? We can plan to take breaks when we know we tend to feel tired. We can plan meals to give us energy when we need it. Today, let's honor our personal rhythms.

I listen to the rhythms inside me for guidance and direction.

Self-Talk *July 15*

WE MAY SCOLD OUR CHILDREN IF they "talk back" to us. We may cast a cold eye on a spouse who uses a sharp tongue. We may hang up the phone if a friend or lover mistreats us. But, oh the abuse we sometimes take from ourselves!

Let's treat the inner critic that constantly judges, frightens, and attacks us with the same assertiveness we show others. Today, let's say no more! No more beating ourselves up. No more negative thinking. No more self-doubt. Let's teach our inner critic to speak lovingly and supportively.

If the messages we are giving ourselves don't support our desires, we need to change them. Don't tolerate negative thoughts from yourself. You deserve better. Rather than letting your inner voice "get smart" with you, get smart about it.

I talk to myself with love and respect.

Oh Happy Day! *July 16*

THE OLD GOSPEL SONG GOES "OH HAPPY Day" and celebrates the joy of knowing God and being alive. No matter what problems we face today, we can find joy and peace if we turn to our Higher Power.

We don't have to join a religion or make a public declaration, but we can open ourselves to the idea of a spiritual power. For example, we can choose to believe in the forces of nature. Many tribes and clans worshiped gods they believed ruled the sun, moon, rain, and wind. Their reverence of nature and closeness to the earth inspired and comforted them. Or we can have faith in the life force that we feel beating in our hearts and witness in our children's faces.

We don't have to name or categorize God, we can simply be grateful and celebrate love and beauty. Believe and you will experience joy.

Today is a happy day because I have faith in the power of love and in myself!

SELF-EXPRESSION IS HOW WE COMMUnicate our personalities to the world. We don't communicate only through speech. Everything we say or do tells people about us. We express ourselves through our clothes, furnishings, and other possessions. We express ourselves through our choice of vocations and hobbies. We also express ourselves by the company we keep. These are external displays of what is inside of us: our ideas, opinions, and aspirations.

Let's look around and determine if we are expressing ourselves in the best way for us. If we aren't representing ourselves in the way we would like, we can change. Let's be sure that we are clear with our communication so that people see what is truly inside of us.

Self-expression is a daily choice. Today, choose to express your highest self.

I creatively express what is inside of me.

Our Strengths *July 18*

PEOPLE OF COLOR OFTEN HEAR about what ills face our communities, but rarely does society or the media focus on our strengths. It is healthy for us to acknowledge the problems we have personally and collectively so that we can address them. It is also healthy and affirming to recognize our strengths.

Many of us have rich spiritual lives that connect us to God, nature, and humanity. Our spiritual traditions give us strong values that help us make moral judgments. Many of us have a sound sense of family. Though we have our occasional "fall outs," we gain strength from bonding with all generations of our families. Our familial love often stretches to neighbors and friends who need our assistance. We are generous people.

We have gained immense reserves of strength from the tribulations our ancestors suffered, and we will become stronger from the hardships we face today. We are people with much power. We can use our love, consideration, understanding, faith, and hope to see us through any crises. Call on your internal reservoirs of strength and be proud.

The strength of my people is within me.

Diligence *July 19*

Persistence and a positive attitude are necessary ingredients for any successful venture. —DOUGLAS WILDER

THERE IS PROFIT IN PERSISTENCE, not only in terms of financial gains, but in personal reward. We receive from life exactly what we put into it. No more. No less. Earnest, continual, energetic efforts earn success.

We must be diligent in our efforts to advance ourselves in life—in our work, relationships, health, and well-being. If we have faith and work hard, we will succeed. We can look at YoYo Ma, Gloria Estefan, and Ben Nighthorse Campbell as examples of how perseverance and confidence pay. We are capable of achieving whatever our hearts desire.

I am diligent in my pursuits. I know success awaits me.

MANY PSYCHOLOGISTS THINK DREAMS are the window to our unconscious minds and our souls. Dreams offer us a key to know what our deepest selves are thinking. If we are not in touch with what we want or what we know, we can turn to our dreams for guidance. What are your hopes, fears, wishes? Turn to the enlightening images of your dreams.

Poets and writers use dreams for inspiration, but anybody can access the creative information in dreams to apply to their daily lives. Many people find it helpful to write down their dreams as soon as they awaken. Some even keep notebooks by their beds so they can record their dreams immediately.

Explore your dreams. Open a window to another world. There are lessons waiting for you there.

I venture into the discerning world of my dreams and bring back immeasurable knowledge about myself.

Managing Stress *July 21*

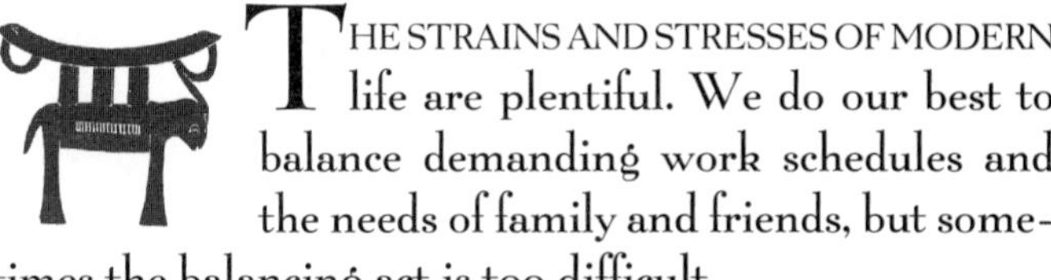

THE STRAINS AND STRESSES OF MODERN life are plentiful. We do our best to balance demanding work schedules and the needs of family and friends, but sometimes the balancing act is too difficult.

We can help ourselves manage stress by not taking on more than we can handle. Sometimes people of color overcompensate for racist stereotypes and try to convince the world that we are talented, professional, capable, worthy people. We are, but by buying into the idea that we have to prove our worth, we make ourselves tense. We don't have to act superhuman to confirm we are human.

We also can help ease our anxiety by setting boundaries for what we will and won't allow. On the days when it feels like we have only one last nerve and everyone wants to wear on it, boundaries can protect us.

Don't let outer forces create inner discord. We are valuable human beings. We don't have to do or say anything to establish our worth with God or with people who love us. Today, we can simply allow ourselves to be. We may not be able to completely eliminate anxiety from our lives, but we can stop stressing ourselves.

I handle stress with ease.

Self-reliance *July 22*

We must stop blaming 'Whitey' for all our sins and oppressions and deal from situations with strength.

—ADAM CLAYTON POWELL JR.

WE MUST STOP BLAMING WHITE people, "the system," our parents, spouses, or anybody else we fault for where we are. Yes, there is racism. Yes, there is abuse, but the only way we will get anywhere in this life is to accept responsibility for our lives.

We must do all we can to combat racism on legal, business, and social fronts. But the most crucial battle goes on in our minds. We must banish harmful thoughts about ourselves and stop thinking like victims. We must acknowledge when and how we keep ourselves down. Nobody can make us feel inferior unless we let them. We must take responsibility and control our decisions and actions. Then we will have freedom to move forward and achieve whatever we want.

I am a powerful, responsible person who accepts accountability for my actions and always moves toward my goals.

Co-dependency *July 23*

THE TERM "CO-DEPENDENCY" ORIGInally applied to a person—the alcoholic's mate, for example—who was emotionally dependent on someone who was dependent on a substance. Now, the term is more broadly applied to people who are dependent on others for their feelings about themselves. A woman who tolerates abuse from a man because "it's better than being alone" could be said to be co-dependent. Another example of co-dependency is a man who can't make even a simple decision without first consulting his parents.

Co-dependency describes emotional immaturity and uncertainty—people who can only see themselves in the eyes of others. Co-dependency is a learned behavior, which can be unlearned. With love and commitment to ourselves, we can teach ourselves to trust ourselves and turn inward for validation. It feels great for others to show they value us, and we shouldn't turn away from support. However, when the only way we can feel good about ourselves is by pleasing others, then we're in trouble.

Spend today loving yourself. You and those you love will benefit.

I don't need others to validate me. I know my worth.

Self-Pity — *July 24*

BAD THINGS SOMETIMES HAPPEN TO good people. When they do, we rack our minds searching for a reason. We want to know "why us?" Perhaps there is an answer, and knowing the answer will console us. But we mustn't stay so wrapped up in our search that it turns into self-pity.

When we experience tragedy, pitying ourselves is a natural response. However, pity develops a choke hold on our soul if we hang on to it too long. Pity is like steaming soup that warms us for a while, but if we sit too long over our bowls, the soup curdles and becomes sour; if we eat too much, we'll get sick. The spirit sours on a steady diet of self-pity.

If we have suffered a misfortune, we shouldn't try to rush the grief process. We can just be aware that there will be a time when we realize self-pity increases the sadness. There will be a time to let go of pity and take action. We *can* make things better for ourselves. What can we do to better our circumstances? What options and choices do we have?

I know when to let go of pity and move forward.

Dual Heritage *July 25*

Because I am neither culturally pure Japanese nor pure American does not mean I am less of a person. It means I have been enriched with the heritage of both.

—JEANNE WAKATSUKI HOUSTON

WE WHO HAVE DUAL HERITAGES HAVE the best of both worlds: the American ethic of individual freedom and the spiritual connection of our ethnic backgrounds. We have learned much from both and blended them into a unique culture that integrates both legacies.

Trying to balance both our identities can be stressful, and sometimes we may wonder if it is worth it. Trying to fit into the melting pot can cause us to wear a mask that hides our true self. When we hide our true selves, we become stifled, oppressed, and stress-ridden.

But, we don't have to give up a part of ourselves to fit into American society. Our dual heritage is what makes us special. Let's look deep into ourselves and select a part of our cultural background that we love or cherish and share it with a person of a different cultural background. Our dual heritage is one of our gifts.

I celebrate my dual heritage. It is a blessing.

Standing Up for Ourselves *July 26*

Step up and let yourself be heard and seen. —ALEX REYES

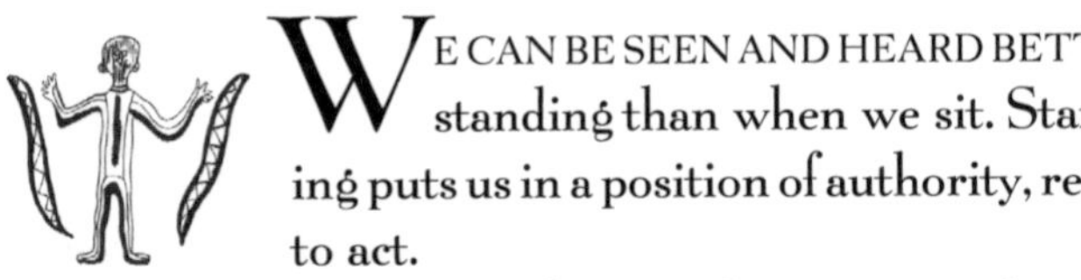

WE CAN BE SEEN AND HEARD BETTER standing than when we sit. Standing puts us in a position of authority, ready to act.

If we don't stand up for ourselves, no one else will. It is our duty and our right to protect ourselves and speak up for ourselves.

Today, let's respect ourselves. Let's act like the proud human beings our ancestors know we are. Let's show the world we mean what we say. Don't be afraid. Be strong. Be confident. Stand up and be counted.

I stand up for my beliefs and my values.

ALCOHOLISM IS A DEADLY DISEASE that affects too many of our people. Many people think alcoholics are "bad" people who need to learn self-control. Addiction to alcohol has nothing to do with morality or will power. Alcoholics are people who have a physiological and emotional dependency on alcohol. They can never learn "to drink like normal people."

Many support groups, particularly Alcoholics Anonymous, help people break their addiction to alcohol and drugs. We can help friends and loved ones who have drinking problems by telling them we are concerned and are aware of their out-of-control behavior. We can offer to direct them to treatment centers or programs, but we can't force them to get help. If we are in a relationship with someone who is drinking themselves to death, we can get help for ourselves through Al-Anon and other support groups.

We can educate ourselves about alcohol and drug abuse to stop the silence, end the shame, and break the cycle. We can take action against the forces that cause our people to turn to drink. Alcohol is not the answer. Love, faith, self-respect, and courage are the tools that build a foundation for ourselves and our community.

I do not hide behind drugs or alcohol. I face life head on.

PEOPLE WHO GROW UP WITH A PARENT who is an alcoholic often develop common characteristics that they carry into adulthood. Some traits of adult children of alcoholics are low self-esteem; procrastination; loyalty, even to people who don't deserve their allegiance; difficulty being intimate and honest with others; extreme need for validation and approval; no frame of reference for appropriate behavior; being over-responsible or under-responsible; being judgmental and critical of themselves and others; feeling different from others; and needing to be in control.

For those of us raised in alcoholic or other dysfunctional families, reviewing our history helps us see how it affects our present lives. These traits aren't permanent. Al-Anon, Ala-Teen, and other self-help programs can benefit people who were or are affected by other's addictions. With self-love and help from supportive friends and our Higher Power, we can learn to minimize the destructive patterns we learned from the chaos, fear, and shame in our families of origin.

I let go of bad habits I developed in my family of origin and commit myself to learning new, healthy ways of being.

Envy and jealousy, to the maturing Navajo woman, are the most harmful of all the diseases and the most self-destructive.

—MARY MOREZ

ENVY IS SELF-DESTRUCTIVE BECAUSE we begrudge the possessions or traits of others, discounting our unique strengths. When we focus all our energy on what others have, we allow our talents and abilities to wither from neglect.

We need to change our perceptions of ourselves. We must let go of envious feelings and focus on building ourselves up. We must wish others well and then concentrate on what we have to offer. We are endowed with many characteristics for which we can be grateful and proud.

Today, rather than seeing ourselves as "have nots," let's view ourselves as "haves." We all have equal amounts of love, blessings, and good will available to us. We all have gifts that make us special. Let's transform the emotional energy of envy into the power of achievement.

I have a bottomless supply of good will and charity.

If Only — *July 30*

"IF ONLY" ARE TWO OF THE SADDEST words in the world. They speak of regret, missed opportunities, and loss. "If only" begs the question: "What would have become of me if I would have made a better choice?" If only... I had accepted that job... married the other person... stayed in school.

Life goes on, and we can't move with it if we are wallowing in the sorrow of "if only." These words can become an excuse to stay stuck in our misery and remorse. We may start to believe that since we didn't do whatever we think would have made things better for us it's too late to help ourselves.

Hindsight gives us all perfect judgment. In the present, it will not always be easy to take the right path, and we may stumble along the way. However, if we accept responsibility for our actions and make a commitment to keep moving forward, it's never too late. Perhaps one opportunity is lost forever, but there will be others. We must let go of past mistakes and focus on what we can do now that will make us proud and satisfied.

With conscious action we can lessen the "if onlys" of our life.

I know what I need to do today so I won't have to say "if only" tomorrow.

MANY OF US THINK LOVE IS THE baby-don't-leave-me-I-can't-live-without-you lyrics heard in popular music. We think love is sweaty palms, butterflies in the stomach, obsession with him or her. When we are first enchanted with someone, love is all passion, romance, and excitement. These feelings aren't wrong: attraction and desire for others is healthy and wonderful. However, for love to last it must move beyond the feelings of infatuation.

Passion ebbs and flows. We must be willing to hang in there during the time we don't feel very passionate. We must be willing to work to cultivate the relationship. Solid marriages and mature relationships are based on commitment and trust. We must listen to our mates, children, and friends. We must be there for them. Every day we must make the decision to practice the act of love.

I choose to love and be loved.

Women can have 'masculine' characteristics (action, courage, rage, ambition), while men can be tender and compassionate. This complexity makes them more interesting in both real life and literature. —ISABEL ALLENDE

IN CHINESE COSMOLOGY YIN REPRESENTS feminine principles and yang reflects the masculine. Separate, they are incomplete; together, they produce all that comes to be.

The Fang people of Gabon, Africa, demonstrate the interconnected relationship between male and female by equating hot, day, sun, and sky with masculinity, and cold, night, moon, and earth with femininity. Two opposites of the same whole.

Men and women should celebrate their sexuality, their maleness and their femaleness. Each gender offers remarkable qualities to the other. Just as the sun is not greater than the moon, neither sex's traits are more valuable than the other's. We also should honor masculinity in women and femininity in men. We need both parts to be human.

I celebrate my maleness and my femaleness.

Pamper Day *August 2*

TODAY IS ANOTHER DAY DESIGNATED for self-care. Let's use this Pamper Day to get in touch with our deepest feelings and desires. We can pamper ourselves with all the love, attention, affection, and approval for which we yearn. We can treat ourselves like we would our best friend. If we have been "down in the dumps," we can cheer ourselves. If we have achieved a great accomplishment, we can celebrate. If we feel a little lost, we can ask God or a wise friend for direction. Today, let's give ourselves whatever we need.

While certain days in this book are selected as Pamper Days, we needn't wait for one of these days. Trust yourself. You're the best judge of what you need. Anytime you feel like you need a day to "treat" yourself, take it.

I nurture myself and watch myself blossom.

Breaking Habits *August 3*

IF WE REPEATEDLY FIND OURSELVES IN the same situation—getting involved in destructive relationships, overextending ourselves at work, spending beyond our budgets—we can be aware that we've learned some bad habits that need to be unlearned.

To break a habit, we must discover what keeps us hooked into duplicating behavior we no longer want to repeat. We can ask ourselves: What is the trigger that causes us to repeat behavior? Are we attracted to partners who remind us of a parent? Do we spend money when we are depressed? Do we overeat or drink when we are lonely? These are clues that will help us get at the root of habitual behavior. Habits are like dandelions: If we don't nip them at the root, they will come back in full force.

I weed unhealthy habits from my mind and make room for a garden of lovely flowers.

WE SEE OFFENSIVE STEREOtypes of people of color every day—in movies, television shows, advertisements, and books. A steady barrage of such insults can make it difficult to feel good about ourselves. Our children are especially vulnerable to such images.

We must combat negative messages about people of color from within and without. We can write to filmmakers, editors, and corporations and insist on more realistic portrayals. We can vote for politicians who support equal treatment for all. But, most important, we need to protect ourselves and our children from internalizing such beliefs.

If we believe stereotypical lies about our people, we must rid ourselves of them. We must reject the mentality that we are helpless victims. We must reclaim our sense of responsibility and actively fill our hearts and minds with self-love. We must learn the truth about our people and ourselves. We have great power to affect our lives and situations around us. We are *not* stereotypes and we don't have to accept them. Let's teach ourselves and our youths to believe in ourselves. Let's destroy negative stereotypes.

I know the truth about myself so I do not allow stereotypical characterizations around me or my children.

⁘ ⁘ ⁘ ⁘ ⁘ ⁘ ⁘ ⁘ ⁘ ⁘ ⁘ ⁘ ⁘ ⁘ ⁘ ⁘ ⁘

LIFE'S JOURNEY IS FRAUGHT WITH PITfalls, steep hills, quick turns, and deep valleys. Sometimes we are slow to see the signs that would alert us to a change in the path. However, we can help ourselves by being prepared for the unexpected changes that come our way.

We also can prepare ourselves for change by educating ourselves. Education broadens our resources for solutions. The more we know, the more tools we have to apply when something goes wrong. Education also helps us stay on track. When we are educated, we are aware. If we think we see a problem heading our way, we can do something to nullify it before it happens. Education prepares us by arming us with knowledge.

The only thing we can count on in life is change; nothing is constant. We always will face surprises; however, we can better deal with surprises by being flexible and open. Rigid, narrow-minded thinking keeps us stuck in ruts. Let's open our minds to new ideas and philosophies and be willing to explore new territories.

Be aware and watch for signs on the road of life. Let the signs prepare you for the next step.

I prepare myself with knowledge, courage, and faith.

Community *August 6*

Try to do something for your people—something difficult.

—WINNEBAGO LESSON

SOME OF US GREW UP IN MIDDLE-CLASS neighborhoods with well-manicured lawns, feeling little connection to our poorer brothers and sisters. Some of us were raised in ghettos, barrios, or on reservations but moved when we could afford to. Whatever our situation, we are blessed when we are able to care for ourselves and our families in comfortable homes on safe streets.

We can share this blessing with others who aren't so fortunate. We don't have to move into neighborhoods where we don't want to live. But we can give our time to the people who do live there. We can go into the ghetto, barrio, or reservation and help make them better places to establish businesses and raise families. We can be muscle for people who have little strength and speak for people who have forgotten their voices.

No matter what the physical distance between us and our community, we are still a part of it. We share in its failures as well as its successes.

I take one step toward improving my community and know that by helping others I am helping myself.

FEELING GUILTY AFTER DOING WRONG is a sign of a healthy conscience. Only sociopaths never feel remorse. It's natural and desirable for us to feel guilty when we lie to, steal from, or hurt other people. Feeling guilty lets us know we have broken our bond of trust with others. We also will feel guilty because we have betrayed ourselves, for when we do harm to others, we do harm to ourselves. We are all connected.

We can use guilty feelings to help clean up our acts and amend our behavior. However, we needn't torture ourselves for making a mistake. Beating up on ourselves and telling ourselves what bad people we are will not motivate us to be better, it will only make us feel worse. We can honestly acknowledge the wrong we have done and, if possible, fix it. If it's not possible to repair the damage, we can learn from this mistake so we don't repeat it.

Guilt isn't a pleasant emotion, but it is a sign of a healthy psyche.

I acknowledge my errors willingly, knowing that I am a lovable, worthwhile person.

CHI IS THE ENERGY OR LIFE FORCE WE all have within us. Some Chinese people believe an imbalance of *chi* is what causes illness. *Chi* has a variety of functions, but its primary duties are to fuel and harmonize the body.

The Chinese way, like other Asian cultures, is the way of balance and moderation. We can benefit from this philosophy. Let's honor the *chi* that is within us by taking care of our bodies, spirits, and minds and maintaining balance. Let's eat properly, exercise moderately, get plenty of rest, and keep emotionally balanced.

I live in balance and harmony.

IF WE WERE ABUSED OR DISCRIMINATED against, we may have grown up learning to distrust others. But we have to trust to make it in this life. We must trust ourselves, God, and other people.

Sometimes we let past experiences color our current relationships. If in the past lovers, friends, or family members offended us, we might find it hard to believe that people we know now won't also hurt us. We can learn to analyze current situations for similar patterns, but it's not fair to compare people. We can discern that we are attracted to certain types of men or women who could break our hearts, and we can learn to avoid those types of people. But just because a past love cheated on you doesn't mean your present sweetheart will. Just because a former co-worker set you up doesn't mean your current colleagues will double-cross you.

We must learn to judge people by their actions. We can determine if the people we are involved with now are trustworthy and if they are, give them our trust. Sincere people deserve our trust and respect, just as we deserve relationships with dependable, considerate people.

I trust myself to know the difference between trustworthy people and untrustworthy people.

The Power of Prayer *August 10*

When we recognize where our power truly comes from, we are blessed.
—BEN VEREEN

PRAYER WORKS. EXACTLY HOW IT works . . . well, there are different opinions about that. We can believe in a Higher Power and the ability of that power to work miracles in our lives. However, communing with spiritual forces ultimately demands some action on our part. God isn't a spiritual Santa or fairy godmother who's going to make all our dreams come true. We can turn to our Higher Power for solace, wisdom, and comfort, but we are responsible for making our dreams come true.

Prayer allows us to focus and ask for guidance on how to proceed with our lives. We pray and then act according to the will of our Higher Power. We can think of prayer as a type of therapy—a treatment for spiritual woes. It is an opportunity to quiet and focus ourselves and a time to commune with a force greater than we.

Prayer is an act of faith. We can trust that universal love will guide and direct us. We can trust that what we are experiencing is for our highest good. Through prayer, we can discover where our power comes from.

I pray with faith in my Higher Power and trust in my ability to act.

LANGUAGE IS AN IMPORTANT TOOL of communication. The person who commands language commands power.

With our words, we can bridge spaces between ourselves and others or cause gaps to widen. With our words, we can make peace or make war. Therefore, we should be careful about the words we choose and make sure we know what they mean. We also should be certain that others understand what we are saying to them. We can ask them to repeat back in their own words what we have said. We can listen to their replies to our statements, and if it seems they have misinterpreted, we can explain ourselves.

To be able to share ourselves is a gift. We don't have to become fancy linguists who dazzle people with our command of the language. Carefully chosen words, spoken from the heart, are the best poetry there is.

My words are powerful tools I use with care and confidence.

DIFFERENT CULTURES HAVE DIFFERENT standards of beauty. Some cultures associate heavy bodies with beauty. To them stoutness means prosperity and fertility. Other cultures admire thinness for its implied sacrifice and discipline. Standards of beauty also change with time.

Modern society would have us believe that beauty comes only in Barbie and Ken sizes and shapes. Let's not allow the public's passing fads to dictate our notions of beauty. Society's taste is fickle: What's in style one minute is out of fashion the next. People with virtues like integrity, kindness, and generosity are always beautiful.

My beauty transcends fads and fashions.

Laugh at Yourself *August 13*

BEING ABLE TO LAUGH AT OURSELVES when we mess up is a sign of healthy self-esteem. We don't have to take our foibles so seriously. Just because we make mistakes doesn't mean we are bad people. Errors simply demonstrate our humanity. Laughing at ourselves loosens our inhibitions and keeps us humble. When we're not so caught up in pretending that we know everything, we are free to learn from our mistakes. We can even make a game out of it. We can put a quarter in a jar every time we say the word "oops." We can use silly names—like "boo-boo" and "oh-oh"—for mistakes. Rather than being ashamed, we can tell a friend or co-worker about the funny fumbles we make.

We can have a good laugh at our own expense today. We'll be all the wiser for acknowledging our errors.

I am mature enough to laugh at myself.

Heroes *August 14*

No person among us desires any other reward for performing a brave and worthy action, but the consciousness of having served his nation. —THAYENDANEGEA (JOSEPH BRANT)

MANY OF US GREW UP ADMIRING CARtoon superheroes like Wonder Woman and Superman. It's unfortunate that the media didn't use people of color to reflect such noble behavior. Luckily, many of us had elders we looked up to. Our elders didn't have to leap over tall buildings or run faster than a speeding train to be heroes. We admired them for their strength, wisdom, and compassion.

We, too, can be heroes to some youngster by modeling meritorious behavior. It's valiant enough simply to do right by people and ourselves. We can be heroes by achieving our dreams, taking care of ourselves, our children, and our communities. We might not be the stuff legends are made of, but we can be people who are honored and respected for our principles. Isn't that what a real hero is?

I heroically stand up for my rights, honor my values, and serve my purpose.

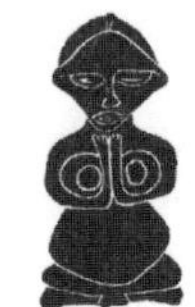

AFRICAN SLAVES MADE UP SONGS that used biblical references to communicate to each other. These "call and response" songs hid their thoughts and feelings from the masters. Spirituals later became a solid tradition among African-Americans. People sang "We Shall Overcome" and other songs to uplift them during the civil-rights movement.

Gospel songs give people strength, hope, and joy: qualities that we can always use more of. They are affirmations put to song, reaffirming that God loves us, we will make it, and we'll be OK. Preachers across the country depend on choirs to help inspire and invigorate their congregations, but we don't have to be in church to receive the benefit of the spiritual.

Whether "Amazing Grace," "Holy, Holy, Holy," or "My Heart Is Still Rejoicing," we too can sing spirituals to connect us to our Higher Power. Today, we can sing songs of faith, hope, survival, and strength. We can allow these songs to move our spirits to greater heights.

I lift my voice and sing what is in my heart.

WHEN WE ARE STRESSED, TIRED, OR worried, a deep breath is better than a cocktail, a joint, or a piece of cheesecake. If we are anxious or afraid, we sometimes breathe shallowly or hold our breaths for extended periods. Breathing relaxes us and sends oxygen to our brains so we think better.

Here's an exercise: Breathe deeply and imagine that you inhale tranquility and love along with clean, fresh air. As the air fills your lungs, let calmness wash away negative, depressing thoughts. Exhale anxiety and fear and feel yourself becoming rejuvenated. Do this ten times, all the while telling yourself soothing, peaceful thoughts. Allow yourself to take a break from your active pace and let go of worry and doubt.

If you have a hard time remembering to breathe deeply, create a trigger to remind you to breathe. Post a little note that says "breathe" on your bathroom mirror, refrigerator door, or by your computer. You could establish a pattern where you stretch and take a deep breath at the beginning of every hour. Or you could make it a habit to inhale and exhale deeply before you answer your telephone.

Serenity is only a breath away.

With each breath, I grow more calm and relaxed.

Body-Mind Connection *August 17*

...the ideal samurai, *or* bushi, *is a versatile man, who would use both his body and his mind to serve his fellow man.*

—DAVID HSIN-FU WAND

ANCIENT MYSTICS KNEW THERE WAS A connection between what people think and feel. Modern medical science is starting to acknowledge that how we react to the events in our lives affects our physical as well as our mental health. Stressful, negative thoughts can cause aches and diseases.

On the other hand, our physical reactions affect our mental condition. For instance, when we exercise, laugh, or make love, our brains release chemicals—called endorphins—that raise our spirits and make us feel good. After a shot of endorphins, we are more likely to think positively.

T'ai chi, karate, judo, yoga, and African martial arts are disciplines that help people get in touch with the connection between their minds and bodies. The movement and supreme concentration needed for these exercises train people to listen to their whole selves.

Like our ancestors, we can be aware of the link between our bodies and our minds. We can listen to our minds and bodies and see what they have to teach us.

I honor the connection between my mind and body.

Setting Goals *August 18*

ONE IMPORTANT STEP WE CAN TAKE to improve our lives is to set a goal. Whatever we want—stronger relationships, more interesting work—we can achieve.

When we set a goal, we make a decision about what we want in life and set a course for action. Without a goal, we are more apt to float aimlessly through life and have decisions made for us. Setting goals gives us a way to gauge our progress. When we set a goal, we create a target to aim for, a path to follow.

Our goals don't have to be carved in stone. As we mature, our goals will change. We can adjust our plans to achieve our new goals.

Setting goals and developing strategies to meet those goals proves to us that we are serious. We show ourselves that we care. We give ourselves confidence to proceed.

I set a goal and "keep my eyes on the prize."

Let Go and Let God *August 19*

LETTING GO CAN BE DIFFICULT. WE have had to fight so much and work so hard to get ahead that often we don't know when or how to let go. Perhaps we are afraid that if we stop holding on so tightly, we'll lose control.

When we turn things over to God, we don't just shrug our shoulders and give up. Turning our lives over to God is not a passive act; we don't sit back and wait for gifts to fall from the heavens. Letting go is a forceful, positive action. We put things in God's hands and work on the things we can control.

Turning over to God also opens us up to new ways of handling problems. We get so busy doing things the same old way that we lose sight that there might be a better way. There is a powerful feeling that comes with giving our problems to our Higher Power. We gain insight and become empowered. Today, we can let go and let God and know that we are acting in our best interests.

I let go of ineffective old patterns and turn to God for direction.

WE ARE SOMETIMES AFRAID OF THE truth, afraid that telling another the truth or learning it ourselves will be painful. Truth may, indeed, bring pain, but it also will bring wisdom. We must not let the fear of pain prevent us from seeking truth. We must be willing to experience the uneasiness of the truth if we want to receive the accompanying insights. When we sacrifice reality to avoid fear, we harm ourselves worse than we would ever hurt from knowing the truth. We must always make living in truth our number one objective.

To help us face our fears, we can change our perceptions. We can remind ourselves that no matter what discomfort we or others feel from knowing the truth, there's always beauty in the truth. Enlightenment, love, and power are results of living truthfully.

Whatever we are afraid of knowing, we can allow ourselves to know today. We can be assured that everyone benefits from truth. Knowing the truth is what sets us free.

I live in reality and truth.

The future is in the present. Look and see for yourself.

—THICH NHAT HANH

AFFIRMATIONS ARE POSITIVE STATEments of things we want to be, do, or have expressed in the present tense. Affirmations work by changing our thinking, which changes our feelings and behaviors. If we believe we are loving, we will act more loving.

We don't say affirmations and wait for wonderful things to happen. Affirmative thought is just one tool in the process. We pray, meditate, say affirmations, and then take action.

We also can write affirmations. When saying or writing affirmations, always use positive language. Don't say "I am no longer a selfish person" without adding "I now give freely and joyously." We don't want to reinforce the negative; affirmations are to "make firm" positive thoughts.

Here are some affirmations you might want to try: "I communicate honestly and effectively." "I have all the love I need inside myself, with plenty to give others." "I love, accept, and appreciate myself exactly as I am." "The spirit of God works through me."

I affirm myself with every thought and deed.

Focus on the Positive — *August 22*

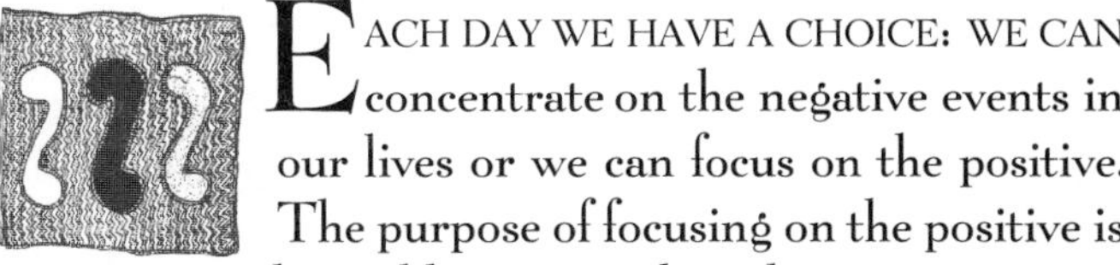

EACH DAY WE HAVE A CHOICE: WE CAN concentrate on the negative events in our lives or we can focus on the positive. The purpose of focusing on the positive is not to ignore the problems in our lives, but to use positive energy to attack them. By looking for opportunities and facing issues with hope and confidence, we can tackle anything that comes our way.

We can use the power of positive thinking in all our affairs. We can transform our relationships by having confidence in ourselves and esteem for others. When we think well of ourselves, we treat others with regard, and they respond with respect. If we are having a bad day at work, we can shift our focus to what is working for us and how we can use the knowledge gained from each experience.

Negative thinking only begets negative actions. We can choose to give energy only to positive thoughts. Let's optimistically face the day and watch the power of positive thought in action.

I think constructive, useful thoughts.

WE DON'T HAVE TO AGREE WITH OR approve of people to have compassion for them. Having compassion simply means we are aware of their misfortune and empathize. If we are disgusted with the man begging for change on the street, we can shift our frame of reference and use our feelings to help him. Rather than reprimand him, we can treat him with dignity. It could be that a kind word is enough to help get him back on the path. Sometimes people need others to have faith in them before they can believe in themselves.

The world is full of people who are disrespectful or irresponsible. We don't have to like them, but we do have to love them.

I have compassion for all my brothers and sisters.

What We Call Ourselves *August 24*

CHICANO, LATINO, HISPANIC, MEXICAN-American, Cuban-American, or Puerto Rican? Native American, American Indian, or Indian? Asian-American, Oriental, Polynesian, Korean-American, Japanese-American, Chinese-American, or Vietnamese-American? African-American or black? Does it really matter what we are called?

It's healthy to have a dialogue about what we call ourselves, and it's politically savvy to be aware of the social implications of names. We can do research and look at the genesis of the names for our people and decide which we prefer. After all, many labels come with distasteful, racist baggage, and we have the right to be called what we choose. However, getting caught up in the "name game" causes us to be sidetracked and lose sight of the much more important issues that face our community. Let's not get so caught up in what we call ourselves that we miss the point. Let's not get so attached to being right about a name that we discount our brothers and sisters who disagree.

We can use one easy name to eliminate the confusion about what we should be called: human beings.

I stay focused on the real issues.

WE MANIFEST AROUND US WHAT WE believe we deserve. Imagine your world is a mirror that reflects everything that is inside of you. If what you see in the mirror is not what you want, you can change it. It is never too late for us to improve our lives.

We start by changing our thought patterns and replacing contemptuous messages with caring affirmations. Once we know in our hearts we are worthy of all the wonderful things life has to offer, we will be able to act in our best interests to achieve them.

We deserve love, peace, understanding, prosperity, and success. We deserve for our lives to reflect all the love, wisdom, and serenity that is within us. What we experience in our lives is what we believe about ourselves in our hearts. Believe in yourself and let the world mirror confidence, trust, and love back to you.

My life reflects all that is good and kind.

IF WE DON'T LIKE WHO WE ARE, WE WILL think others won't like us. So we put on masks we think will be more acceptable to others. We become "The Life of the Party," or "The Person They Can Always Count On." Or to keep others from finding out how bad we think we are inside, we'll put on masks to keep them away. We'll be "The Rebel Without a Cause," or "The Last Angry Man (or Woman)."

What we may find is that not only have we kept others from knowing us, we no longer know ourselves.

The tragedy is that we aren't bad people to begin with. Sometimes parents, the media, society can teach us that we're stupid, lazy, evil, or that we have no worth. We can stop believing these lies. We can take off the masks and discover our real selves.

We may find that the false selves we developed to be liked and accepted really weren't likable to others. And the imitation selves we have created to protect ourselves only isolated and alienated us, contributing to our sense of worthlessness.

The people who love us want to know who we really are. And they will accept us as human beings with flaws and limitations as well as with talents and virtues.

The first person I reveal my true self to is me.

A NEW DAY IS DAWNING. MORE AND more people are realizing that spirituality need not be something they practice once a week. Spirituality can enhance all of our relationships and activities. People of color are deeply spiritual and typically live this philosophy.

However, sometimes we get caught up in today's fast-paced life and lose touch with our spiritual natures. We may experience a wake-up call in the guise of illness or despair. Certainly, the devastation many of our people are experiencing is a sign that they have been disconnected from their sense of God and fellowship with humanity.

If we have temporarily lost our way, we can rekindle our spiritual awareness. We also can help others rediscover the love of others and themselves. A spiritual awakening is a new consciousness, a shift in our system of values. We know we have experienced a spiritual awakening when we live simply and humbly. We have experienced a spiritual awakening when we are concerned about what happens to the rest of our clan and the earth.

I awake my spirituality and live a life based on love and integrity.

WE'VE RECEIVED SOME PERVERSE messages about our sexuality. Common stereotypes cast men as insatiable savages, driven to dangerous ends by lust and women as "geisha girls" or nymphomaniacs. As with other clichés about people of color, sexual stereotypes are a result of ignorance and were designed to minimize our mental capabilities and deny us our humanity.

We've also been taught that men have stronger sexual drives than women and therefore are prone to affairs. First of all, women have just as much right to sexual pleasure as men do. Second of all, this theory is a lie that excuses deceit and irresponsibility. If we profess to practice monogamy, we should be faithful.

We needn't let such stereotypes damage our ideas about sex and feelings about our sexuality. No matter what the media displays, we can know that our sexuality is only one part of our identity. We can enjoy our sexuality to whatever degree feels appropriate for us. We can be passionate and fiery and glory in our sexuality without buying into negative stereotypes.

Let's be lovers of life today. We deserve to live with joy, abandon, and delight.

Without reservation, I accept my God-given right to pleasure.

FUN AND RESPONSIBILITY ARE NOT OPPOsites of each other. Indeed, for an activity to bring us joy it should be done responsibly.

The enjoyment that comes with a good meal or a fine wine quickly turns to sickness and disgust if we overeat or get drunk. The pleasure of a new purchase doesn't last long if it is repossessed because we haven't maintained our finances. The passion that may drive us to engage in unsafe sexual practices won't last as long as the fear of disease or unwanted pregnancy.

The way of balance is moderation and responsibility. We can and should enjoy life—we're not here to complete one chore after another. We are here to learn and love, and our time on this planet can be a wonderful time. Entertainment, laughter, and recreation are good for the soul.

Have some fun today, but do so wisely. Make sure you don't pay for today's fun with tomorrow's problems.

I play with the same principles that guide the rest of my life: awareness, responsibility, and choice.

Minority or Majority? *August 30*

When you realize you are part of the majority, you approach your problem as if odds are on your side rather than odds are against you.

—MALCOLM X

THERE'S A NEGATIVE IMPACT ON OUR psyches when we think of ourselves as minorities. It causes us to think in limited ways. It makes us expect only so much for ourselves. The truth is that, worldwide, people of color *are* the majority. And by the twenty-first century, we'll make up most of the American population.

Let's expand our views about ourselves. Let's stop thinking of ourselves as victims. We are people of great power. We are people that built pyramids, developed mathematics, and charted the stars!

I let go of limiting beliefs. I am a powerful human being with infinite choices.

SOMETIMES WE FEEL A SENSE OF DREAD and anxiety, but don't know why. When we are faced with a real threat—a mugger, for instance—feeling afraid is a healthy reaction. Fear tells us to prepare or protect ourselves.

On the other hand, fear of imagined situations can keep us stuck. Fear of failure and rejection, even of success, can cripple us. Free-floating anxiety is a sign that we have unresolved issues.

The first step for conquering fear is knowing what we are afraid of. The second step is accepting ourselves, even though we are afraid. If we are aware and treat ourselves lovingly, we can learn to handle situations that used to fill us with trepidation. Eating alone in restaurants, introducing ourselves to a stranger, or speaking in front of a group of people, and other daring actions soon will become easier.

We probably always will feel afraid about some things. However, we don't have to let our fear keep us from exploring new worlds. We can face our fears and act in spite of them.

I may be afraid, but I still move forward.

I was a very persistent guy. I had many doors slammed in my face, but I have always followed the purpose of my life. I always did what I had to do. —JOSÉ FELICIANO

DOING WHAT WE HAVE TO DO NO MATter how many doors are slammed in our faces is an excellent definition of courage. It takes a great deal of moral strength to follow our hearts in the face of discouragement and bigotry.

Courage is something our people know much about; our ancestors braved more hardship than we can imagine. From them we inherited a capacity for bravely facing strain and difficulty. We have mettle.

We can solve our community's problems—drug addiction, gang violence, unemployment, poverty, illiteracy—by calling on the courage of those who have gone before us.

I courageously knock on as many doors as it takes to achieve my goals.

SEPTEMBER IS HISPANIC HERITAGE month, which honors the heritage of people of Mexican, Puerto Rican, Cuban, Latin American, and Spanish descent. Latinos have contributed much to the fabric of American life. No matter what our ethnicity, we can commemorate the achievements of people like Antonia Novello, Andy Garcia, Manuel Luján Jr., Oscar Hijuelos, Nancy Lopez, Rita Moreno, Ruben Blades, Raul Yzaguirre, and Federico Peña who triumphed in spite of whatever obstacles they may have faced. They are role models for us all.

This month we can reflect on the strength and tenacity of all oppressed people. We can mourn those who were not able to survive persecution and be grateful for those who endured. We can pay homage to the fortitude, wisdom, faith, and courage our ancestors gave to us by passing the torch to the next generation. We can serve as role models to our youth and make sure they know the price paid for their freedom.

Today, I celebrate the faith and accomplishments of people of color. We all have so much to be proud of!

Forgive Yourself *September 3*

PART OF LIVING IS LEARNING TO FORgive. We forgive others for the wrongs they have done us and forgive ourselves for how we have hurt others and ourselves. Some of us have a hard time forgiving ourselves for making errors, being imperfect...being human. Even if we can pardon our minor foibles, it may be difficult to exonerate ourselves for major grievances. Maybe we committed adultery, battered our spouse, or conned and lied to people who trusted us. We all have committed some act of which we are ashamed.

Part of the way for us to right our wrongs and release our shame is to forgive ourselves. Forgiveness doesn't mean that we pretend we never hurt anybody. Self-forgiveness is the first act toward making amends to others and ourselves. When we forgive ourselves, we allow ourselves to be mere human beings capable of evil, as well as good. We also make a pledge to honor the good inside of us by giving energy to it. We stop torturing ourselves for our mistakes and use positive energy to make amends. We have the right to let go of shameful feelings and move forward.

Today is the day for us to forgive and heal ourselves.

With humility and God's grace, I forgive myself for the mistakes I have made and the harm I have done.

Take a Pass — *September 4*

TO RECLAIM OURSELVES WE MUST learn how to avoid getting hooked into the games people play. Some people subconsciously want us to enable and caretake them. They may intentionally start arguments to make us upset, but it takes two people to play and we don't have to. When the ball is in our court, we can let it sit there. We don't have to pick it up. We don't have to throw it back.

If someone asks us a question we know is designed to set us up, we can answer with "I don't think I want to answer." We can say "This sounds like a trick question, and I don't want to play." We can say "I think I'll pass on that."

If someone starts in with a long "woe-is-me" story and expects us to fix it for them, we can say "oh well." It is not inconsiderate to avoid participating in other people's pity parties. We will actually do them a favor by enabling them to seek their own solutions.

If someone tries to involve you in unhealthy behavior, take a pass.

I protect my boundaries and interact with people in a healthy, straightforward manner.

You have to have a physical, emotional, spiritual, and social balance in your life. You can't get out of whack in one area without affecting the others. —CAROLYN FISCUS

BALANCE IS GIVING ALL PARTS OF OUR lives equal time and energy. When we are in balance, we focus no more on our bodies than we do on our minds or spirits, concentrate no more on work than on play.

Compulsive exercisers—who work their bodies past health into illness and injury—often ruin relationships as well as their health. A workaholic may have a very successful career but not know his or her spouse and children. Focusing on one thing to the detriment of others is not the way of balance.

Balance is our natural state of being. Balance is the key to good health.

I follow the wisdom of my ancestors and maintain balance in my life.

MANY OF OUR PEOPLE SUFFER FROM hypertension, obesity, cancer, and other ailments that result from stress and poor health habits. We need to protect our physical health as much as our mental and spiritual health. On this day, let's focus on our bodies' well-being. Here's a short health quiz: Are we over- or underweight? Do we smoke? Do we exercise? How's our diet? If the answers to these questions point to unhealthy behaviors, let's make a commitment today to take better care of ourselves.

If you smoke, today is the day to quit. Join a smoker's support group or ask friends and family for help, and do it *now.* Recent studies show every cigarette takes seven minutes off your life.

If you have unhealthy eating habits, today is the day to learn more about nutrition. We should eat more grains and fruits and vegetables and less fat and sweets.

If you are a couch potato, today is the day to go for a walk. Walking is free and almost anybody can do it. Regular doctor's visits are also an important part of preventative medicine. Ask your doctor to provide more information about diet and exercise. The best way to fight disease is to prevent disease.

I am fit and well.

The Light *September 7*

光

PEOPLE WHO HAVE NEAR-DEATH EXPERIENCES almost always describe going through some type of tunnel and following a bright light. To them, the light feels warm and unconditionally loving; it is the ultimate being. Many people believe the light is God.

We don't have to wait until we are dying to see the light of God; that light shines within us. We can look for it in our fellows and encourage our brothers and sisters to shine. We also can see the light in ourselves. Today, let's let our talents shine. Let's let our dreams shine. Let's let our ideas shine. Let's let our characters shine.

We can be a beacon to people who are in need of hope and encouragement. People are attracted to us when we shine in God's love. Every living thing turns toward the light.

I radiate the light that is within me.

Spiritual Energy *September 8*

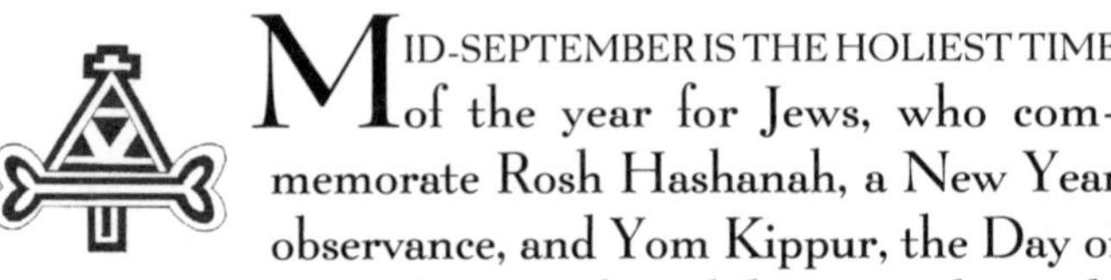

MID-SEPTEMBER IS THE HOLIEST TIME of the year for Jews, who commemorate Rosh Hashanah, a New Year observance, and Yom Kippur, the Day of Atonement. During these High Holidays, Jewish people are encouraged to fast, make amends to relatives and friends, and reflect on their mistakes. Jewish, Christian, Buddhist, or Moslem, we all can benefit from taking time to renew ourselves spiritually.

Just like an appliance that runs on electricity, people need spiritual energy to fuel themselves. People who are low on spiritual energy often describe a feeling of being unconnected or lost. The best treatment for such a feeling is to ground ourselves by renewing our spiritual energy. Plugging into our source.

We can renew our spiritual energy through prayer and meditation. After communing with our Higher Power, we will feel energized and invigorated. We will feel ready to go out and do God's will. Today, let's allow the flow of universal love to rejuvenate us.

I recharge my spiritual batteries and delight in my increased energy.

BEFORE WE CAN READ, WE MUST LEARN the alphabet. Before we can balance a bankbook, we must learn to count. Before we can advance in life, we must know the basics...the ABCs of success.

A stands for awareness. We must be aware of our strengths and weaknesses. We must be aware of what motivates us. We must be aware of what is going on around us.

B stands for belief. We have the ability to realize our dreams, but we won't be able to unless we believe we can. We must believe we can be successful.

C stands for commitment. We must be dedicated to achieving our goals. With commitment and perseverance we will be successful.

Education is continual. We never graduate from the school of life. Today, let's prepare ourselves for the next "grade" by learning our ABCs.

I learn from all my experiences.

Life Force — *September 10*

From Wakan Tanka, the Great Spirit, there came a great unifying life force that flowed in and through all things.... Thus all things were kindred, and were brought together by the same Great Mystery.

—CHIEF LUTHER STANDING BEAR

THE LIFE FORCE IS THE SPIRITUAL power that turns a seed into a flower and a caterpillar into a butterfly. It is the same force that makes our lungs expand, hearts beat, and blood flow. It connects all living things.

Skin color, language, culture—these are outside manifestations of differences. Inside, we are all the same; we are related. We were all born from the same Mother Earth. We need to remember this when we communicate with our brothers and sisters, *even if they don't.*

We can get in touch with our spiritual energy through meditation and prayer, communing with nature, or just sitting quietly. We can let that energy guide us in our relationships, work, and all our affairs. Spiritual practice pushes our egos, doubts, and selfishness out of the way and fills us with a higher knowledge. We are much more effective and peaceful when we allow the life force to work through us.

I am aware of the life force that is in me and the rest of the human family.

TYPICALLY, WE THINK OF EXPLORAtion as discovering new lands and faraway places. But the most exciting adventures begin when we discover who we are. When we know who we are, we can achieve anything. When we know who we are, there is no need to pretend. There is no need to lie.

Today, let's investigate inner spaces. Let's venture into new frontiers. Let's discover ourselves. With God's grace we can find ourselves. As the song says, "I once was lost but now I'm found."

I am an explorer of my hopes and dreams.

BE CREATIVE IN LOOKING FOR WAYS TO be creative. You don't have to write poetry or paint portraits to be inventive—though it's good to pursue those activities if they engage you. Baking, gardening, volunteering, weaving, child-rearing, and entertaining guests are all ways of being creative. Perhaps the easiest way of incorporating creativity into our lives is in problem-solving. If you're having a tough time finding a solution to a problem, turn the situation upside down, inside out, or backwards. Creativity is born out of the courage to risk seeing things in a new way.

Cultivate the components of creativity—play, spontaneity, curiosity, open-mindedness, and wonder. Allow yourself to be kooky, different, even weird. Challenge the norms. Challenge what's expected of you. Transcend the ordinary. Set your mind and spirit free and see what happens.

I give myself permission to create and view my world with a fresh perspective.

Lighten Up *September 13*

WE OFTEN TAKE OURSELVES TOO SEriously. We need to separate ourselves from our problems and responsibilities and treat *them* seriously, not ourselves. Allowing ourselves to lighten up will help us build resilience and strength to persevere during adversity and change. Lightheartedness also gives us a healthy sense of perspective. We are not the center of the universe—the sky will not fall, and the world will not end because of our actions.

In addition, a sense of humor contributes to our emotional well-being. Cultivate humor by looking for the absurd. Laugh at the silliness in politics and world affairs.

Sometimes serious issues leave us flummoxed, and we don't know whether to laugh or cry. Try laughing. Tell jokes, give hugs. Greet everyone you meet with a smile. Take every opportunity to lift your spirits and lighten up. Encourage your friends, family, and coworkers to join you in laughter. Instead of yelling at the guy cutting through traffic, make a funny face at him. Instead of scolding when your child makes a mess, make a game out of cleaning up. Remember: "There's no use crying over spilt milk."

I cheerfully embrace the day before me and smile when I think of the possibilities.

Helping, Not Judging *September 14*

YES, THERE ARE MANY PROBLEMS IN the world and they aren't going to just go away. But there is a fine line between being an activist and being judgmental.

We have no business telling other people how to live. If people's lifestyles are harmful, we can provide education and support so they can help themselves. We can act as role models and demonstrate a healthier way of life. However, if we simply disapprove of other's choices, maybe we should mind our own business.

We would do better to stop judging and start trying to change the situations that cause the problems. For example, if we object to abortions, we could help limit them by educating people about reproduction. We could encourage responsible behavior among girls *and* boys and teach people that actions have consequences. If we disapprove of welfare, we can inspire people to help themselves rather than depending on the government.

We are all responsible for finding solutions, but the answer isn't controlling others. The answer is educating and empowering.

I concentrate on improving situations, not controlling people.

"Here" vs. "There" *September 15*

TRUE, WE ARE ON A JOURNEY AND WE have many goals that we want to accomplish. However, there is no magic finish line when we are perfect and life is free of problems. We must be careful that we don't focus so hard on the destination that we miss the journey. Where we are today is what counts.

Let's take some time to appreciate the gifts we enjoy today. Our situation may not be exactly what we would want for ourselves, but we can still be thankful for what we do have. We can still show our gratitude to the loved ones who serve as our companions on the trip.

If we can't appreciate today, we'll never be able to appreciate tomorrow. If we can't see the blessings we have today, we'll never be content with the gifts we receive tomorrow. There is no end to our journey. Every accomplishment will bring new goals to strive for. Here and now is what matters. It is all we have.

"Here" is where I am today. I'll deal with "there" when I arrive.

Mexican Independence Day *September 16*

THIS HOLIDAY COMMEMORATES THE day in 1810 when a Mexican priest made a call—the *Grito de Dolores*—for Indians and mestizos to rebel against the Spanish. A bloody revolution ensued with Mexicans winning the right to govern themselves in 1821.

When we enter adulthood, we gain the right of self-destination, the right to decide our fates for ourselves. However, sometimes we don't claim our autonomy. If we have allowed others to control us, if we have allowed others to manipulate us, we must free ourselves. We must fight as fiercely for our mental, emotional, and spiritual emancipation as the Mexicans did for their sovereignty.

Today, we can celebrate the bravery of self-determined people everywhere who truly believe in "liberty and justice for all." We can celebrate our right to manage our own lives.

I declare my independence from limiting thoughts and behaviors and go forth into freedom.

AUTUMN IS HARVEST SEASON. A time when farmers celebrate plentiful yields and prepare their fields for spring planting.

We, too, can reap the benefits now of the planning we did earlier. The changes we have made, the risks we have taken, the truths we have found will pay off for us. We can rejoice in the fruits of our labors: an abundant supply of inner resources; infinite, unconditional love from our Creator; and supportive, tender relationships with friends and family members.

We also must prepare ourselves for the crops we want to plant later. What dreams as yet go unaccomplished? What new goals have we set for ourselves? We can be grateful for our achievements and get ready for the challenges ahead. We may experience a cold, hard winter, but if we have prepared, our fields will be ready in the spring.

I reap a bountiful harvest of blessings.

Responsibility *September 18*

The most worthwhile endeavor I have ever undertaken is responsibility for my own life. It's hard and it's worth it.

—LEVAR BURTON

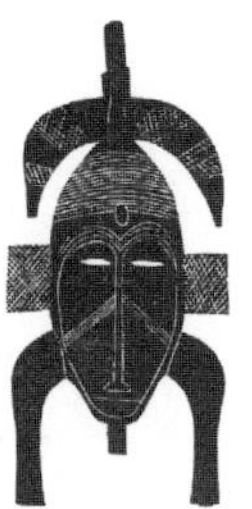

RESPONSIBILITY IS ABOUT HOLDING ourselves accountable for what we manifest in our lives. It's about ownership. Recognizing our ability to choose between right and wrong—our ability to respond. We can examine our lives and determine the best way to handle our problems. We can learn how to be better parents, spouses, and friends. We can learn how to organize ourselves, budgeting both time and money. Whatever we need to fix, it is within our range.

We can do the same with the problems facing the world—environmental damage, hunger, homelessness, illiteracy—and take responsibility for our parts. We can educate ourselves and volunteer our knowledge to help those without. We shouldn't waste valuable time and energy placing blame—either on ourselves or other people. It is much more constructive to focus on what we can do to correct things.

I own my ability to respond.

Evolution — *September 19*

Turning into my own
turning on in
to my own self
at last.

—Lucille Clifton

THE THEORY OF EVOLUTION PROPOSES that creatures that adapt to changing environments will survive and pass along those adaptions to the next generation: survival of the fittest.

We have inherited an ability to adjust and survive from our forefathers and foremothers. We can apply those survival skills to our individual lives. We can continue our survival by learning new information and being willing to change our minds. We don't have to stay stuck with the same old beliefs. We can ensure our survival by changing whatever needs to be changed and fortifying the traits we should keep. Of course, the trick is knowing the difference.

Today, we can choose to transform ourselves into ever higher versions of ourselves or to go the way of the dinosaurs. Evolution or extinction...you decide.

Like the earth and all its creatures, I am constantly evolving.

But, "I can't," is a great barrier in the way. I hope it will soon be removed, and "I will," resume its place.

—MRS. MARIA W. STEWART

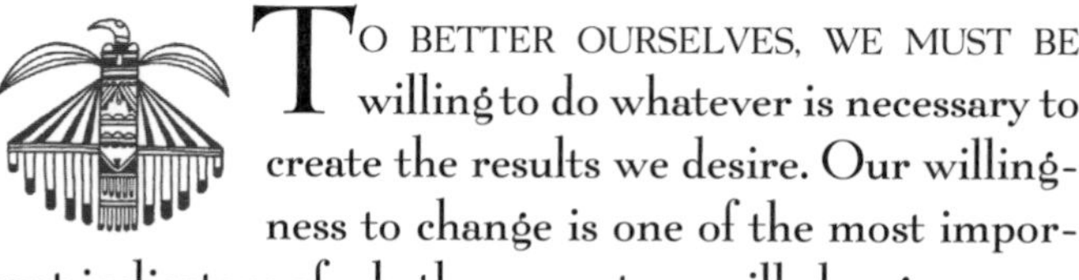

TO BETTER OURSELVES, WE MUST BE willing to do whatever is necessary to create the results we desire. Our willingness to change is one of the most important indicators of whether or not we will change.

Being willing means that we accept responsibility for our lives and make a commitment to doing whatever we have to do. If we must change to have a better life, we do it. If we have to quit drinking, we do it. If we have to move to a different city, we do it. If we have to confront people, we do it. If we have to continue our educations, we do it. If we have to see a therapist, we do it. Being willing means that no matter what we are afraid of, and no matter how hard something is, if it is healthy for us, we do it. We create the lives we want. We can get a better life by being willing and having faith.

I am willing to do the work to get what I want from life.

Think for Yourself — *September 21*

Use your head for something more than a hat rack.

—CONSTANCE RAE WALLS

WHEN WE HAVE TOUGH DECISIONS TO make, we may fall for the lazy man's solution and turn to politicians, community leaders, parents, teachers, bosses, or spouses for answers. We think it will be easier for someone to tell us what to do. But it's not.

We can and should seek counsel and information from others. But we have to make decisions ourselves: We must think for ourselves.

We can't allow other people to run our lives and not suffer for it. Nobody knows better than us what we need to do. If we are confused, we can pray for guidance. We can seek counsel from friends, elders, and books. However, the final decision must be ours.

Today, let's use our heads. We are intelligent, resourceful, creative people. We don't need others to think for us. We can think for ourselves.

I put on my "thinking cap" and find the answers I need.

PEOPLE SAY "GET A LIFE," BUT IT'S NOT that easy. There is no "Life Store" where we can choose from a variety of interesting existences. We can't order a life from home-shopping channels or catalogs. The only way to get a life is to build one.

How do we build a life? The same way we built this country: brick by brick, rail by rail, crop by crop, and day by day.

We must decide what makes life complete and meaningful for us, and then develop that. For example, if we want healthy relationships, we need to cultivate them just as we would a garden. We must give time and attention to the people in our lives for our friendships to blossom. If we want to establish gratifying careers, we must prepare ourselves with the proper and experiences that earn kudos and advance us to the next level.

We can build our lives on a solid foundation of faith, love, and respect.

I am the constructor of my destiny. I use the tools that God has given me to build my life.

The Calling — *September 23*

NOT JUST SHAMANS, PREACHERS, priests, and nuns receive a calling to serve. The world is calling out for us all. We have a purpose to serve, a gift to offer.

We don't have to be ministers to do the Creator's work. We can be waiters, secretaries, teachers, executives, and computer programmers and contribute to the people around us. Oprah Winfrey calls her talk show her ministry. She uses her vocation as a forum to help people heal by regularly hosting programs on child abuse, racism, and mental illness. We can follow her example and ask ourselves what platforms do we have that we can use to reach out to our brothers and sisters.

God has tapped each one of us for a special mission. Listen carefully for your calling. The universe has a unique assignment just for you.

I heed my calling and accept my responsibility to serve.

Family and Self *September 24*

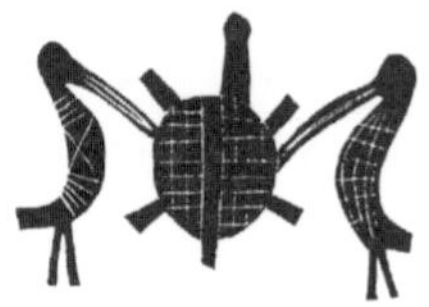

WE ARE OFTEN PULLED IN DIFFERENT directions by our personal desires and our duties to family. Our cultures heavily depended on individuals restricting themselves for the good of the family and the community. Our people may not have survived this far without the full support of all members.

However, our families and communities don't benefit when we deny ourselves the right to grow. No person truly benefits from the limitation of others. If one of us loses his or her sense of identity and self-awareness, then we all lose. All people—mothers, fathers, children—desire to know who they are. We each have a purpose to serve in God's plan. We can't fulfill our mission and do God's will if we never take the time to find out what that is.

We may have to think of compromises to serve the needs of our families and ourselves. We can know ourselves as individuals and still be connected with our families. No matter where we go or what we do, if we share love with our families, they always will be with us.

We serve God, our families, and our communities better by being true to ourselves.

I demonstrate love to my family and to myself.

Self-Loathing *September 25*

Because if I am still bound by my own self-hatred, I am the oppressor onto myself. —ALETÍCIA TIJERINA

SELF-LOATHING IS THE ROOT OF MANY social ills. People of color are told directly and indirectly that there is something wrong with us. Too many of us allowed those messages to seep inside our psyches and came to feel that something about us "just ain't right."

Self-loathing leads to self-destruction. People who hate themselves are terrorized by an internal drive to maliciously punish themselves. They may try to kill themselves by using booze and dope, engaging in unsafe sex, or participating in violent lifestyles.

When you despise yourself, what have you got to lose? A lot. We all do. We can't afford the death of one more young black man, the hopelessness of one more teenage pregnancy, or the despair of another high-school dropout. We can't afford for people to not love themselves enough to believe they could discover a cure for AIDS or lead this country.

You have God-given talents, abilities, and ideas that we need desperately. We need your brilliant, creative solutions. You are the answer. Self-love is the key.

I love and appreciate myself.

Enabling *September 26*

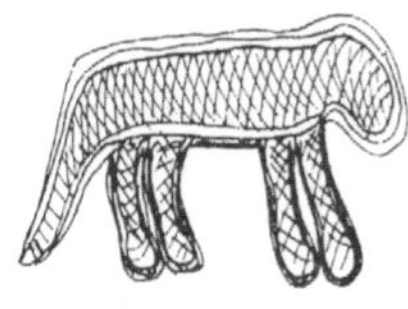

ENABLING IS ALLOWING USUALLY negative behavior by making it easy or possible for another person to do something. For example, the spouse of an alcoholic enables the person's drinking by saying the drinker has the flu when he or she really has a hangover. Enabling also is rescuing people from the trouble their sick behavior causes. People usually won't make the effort to get healthy if they never fully experience the consequences of their actions.

Allowing people to avoid the results of their dysfunction does not help them. If our desire is to help another grow, we can think of empowering, rather than enabling. We can empower addicted or confused people to get the help they need. We can empower children to speak their minds by respecting their opinions so they can grow into more confident, assertive adults. We can empower friends to follow their hearts and make their own decisions.

Let's truly be of service to our friends and loved ones. Let's empower and not enable.

I lovingly empower people to be responsible.

Easy Does It *September 27*

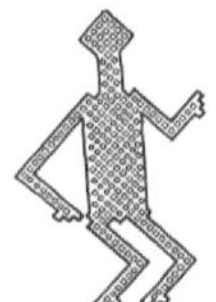

PEOPLE IN ALCOHOLICS ANONYMOUS have an expression to help people who try to rush their recovery: Easy does it. Good advice.

Growing is hard work. Whether we are in a program, undergoing therapy, or exploring alone, self-discovery demands discipline and vigilance. There are times when we have to be diligent to break through denial or to maintain our growth. But we also require "down time" to rejuvenate and refocus. We need time to heal.

Pushing doesn't help. Enlightenment comes when we are ready to receive it. We can't force our growth. Today, let's ease up on ourselves and allow time to rest and recuperate.

Give yourself a break. You've earned it.

I take it easy and experience the spiritual growth that comes with gentleness.

Chances — *September 28*

I'm old and I sit here and I think, what if I had a chance? I know I would make use of it. —LOUISE HIETT

WE HAVE NUMEROUS CHANCES THAT many of our ancestors didn't. Many of them were enslaved, herded off to reservations, or raised in cultures that didn't allow them to grow as individuals.

We have a chance to educate ourselves. It was illegal to teach slaves how to read. Teachers at reservation schools often were more concerned with "civilizing" students than educating them. Hispanic and Asian students regularly fell between the cracks of the school system. Though schools still often ignore and misinform us, we have a far better chance of learning.

We have a chance to live and work where we choose. Segregation and discrimination are no longer acceptable under the law and today, we can take legal recourse if we think our civil rights are being violated.

And we have the chance to be ourselves. There are many social forces designed to keep us from knowing ourselves. However, we don't have the constraints that our elders—especially women—might have faced. We are free, adult people with the ability to decide for ourselves what we believe in and what is right for us.

I make wise use of my chances.

"The Successful Minority" *September 29*

ASIAN-AMERICANS HAVE THE unique experience of being labeled "the successful minority" by some politicians and mainstream press people. The educational and economic achievements of Asian-Americans have been used as a model for other people of color to follow.

This designation insinuates that somehow things came easily to Asian immigrants. During World War II, people of Japanese descent were branded as spies and traitors. More than 120,000 people were taken from their homes and businesses and forced into internment camps. Chinese immigrants virtually built the Transcontinental Railroad and contributed much to America's growth, yet they were discriminated against.

Despite racist assaults, Asian-Americans persevered and those who are successful have every right to feel proud of their accomplishments. However, the "successful minority" characterization is patronizing and negates the damage that racism caused. "The successful minority" is just another stereotype.

No matter what our ethnic background, we shouldn't allow society to label our achievements. We are the only ones who determine our success.

I do not believe stereotypes. I determine issues for myself.

Be True to Yourself — *September 30*

Realizing who you are is your own choice. —ALEX REYES

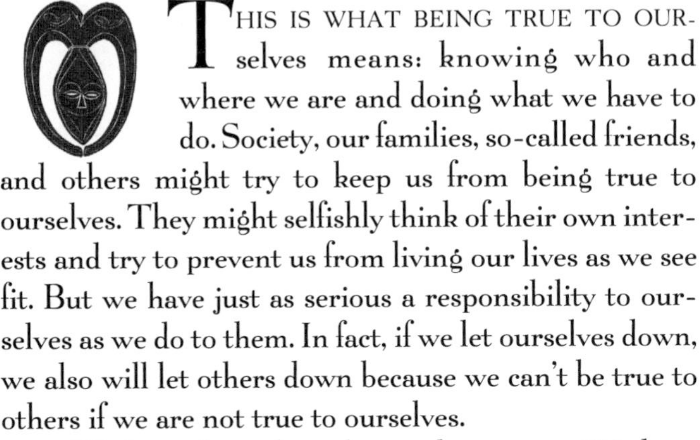

THIS IS WHAT BEING TRUE TO OURselves means: knowing who and where we are and doing what we have to do. Society, our families, so-called friends, and others might try to keep us from being true to ourselves. They might selfishly think of their own interests and try to prevent us from living our lives as we see fit. But we have just as serious a responsibility to ourselves as we do to them. In fact, if we let ourselves down, we also will let others down because we can't be true to others if we are not true to ourselves.

We have the right to live with integrity. We have the right to be who we are. Follow your heart. You know what you have to do.

I assert my right to be my authentic, sacred self. My life and my relationships are the better for it.

Ask the Right Questions *October 1*

Asking the proper question is the central action of transformation—in fairy tales, in analysis, and in individuation... questions are the keys that cause the secret doors of the psyche to swing open. —CLARISSA PINKOLA ESTÉS

UNLESS WE ASK THE RIGHT QUESTION, we won't get the right answer.

The right questions about relationships might be: Am I attracting healthy people? Do I believe I deserve to be treated well? Do I listen to my loved ones? Do I treat people with trust and respect?

The right questions about careers might be: Am I doing work that I enjoy? Am I contributing a useful, needed product? Am I giving good service to my employer or clients?

The right questions about health might be: Do I take responsibility for my mental, physical, and spiritual health? Do I encourage a stressful lifestyle? Do I take time to rejuvenate myself?

Once we ask the questions, answers come, then we can take action to solve our problems. Only you know what the right question is. Ask it and open the door to the perfect answer for you.

I ask myself the proper questions.

Watch and Learn *October 2*

WE CAN LEARN A LOT BY WATCHING what goes on around us. We can observe people who have traits that we would like to have. For example, if we want to be more assertive, we can learn from the woman who demands better service in the restaurant. If we want to be better chefs, we can learn from the grandparent who spends hours in the kitchen, lovingly creating delicious meals. If we want to be better parents, we can learn from the father who patiently twirls his child around the playground for the fifteenth time.

Life is one big classroom. If we open our eyes, lessons are everywhere.

I watch and learn.

Interdependence *October 3*

HUMAN DEVELOPMENT GOES through three phases. First, we are dependent. We need our parents to feed and clothe us. Without their care, we could die. The next phase we enter is independence. We want to stand on our own two feet. We want to do things for ourselves. The final, and most mature, phase is interdependence.

Interdependence is being responsible for ourselves, yet still needing other people. In this phase, we readily acknowledge that we don't know everything. We need and want to learn from others. We realize that human companionship is deeply important to us, however we aren't willing to shortchange ourselves to please others. This phase stresses the give and take between individuals. The teacher and the student count equally.

These stages aren't cut and dried. We fluctuate through them. For example, if we have just divorced, we might want to practice being independent for a while. If we have stubbornly refused to let others help us, we might have to learn how to depend on people.

We must learn to give and take in life. Today, we can reflect on which phase of life we are in and strive for interdependence.

I give and *receive with love.*

Timing — *October 4*

THE BIBLE SAYS "TO EVERYTHING there is a season," a time for everything under the sun, a universal schedule.

There are some things for which there is always a season. The time is always right to assume responsibility for ourselves. The time is always right to share love with people.

If we are confused about whether the time is right for us to take a certain action, we can pray for guidance. We don't have to rush to action. If we are hesitant, there may be a reason. We may have some issues to work through yet. We may be unsure of our decisions. We can wait until our inner voices tell us the time is right.

When we are attuned to our Higher Power, we are always in the right place at the right time. We will know when the time is right.

I am enlightened about the divine plan for my life. When the time is right, I take action.

People Pleasing *October 5*

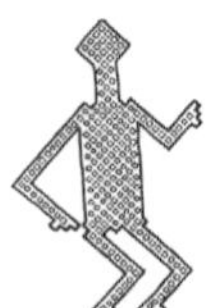

IT IS NOT WRONG TO TRY TO PLEASE people. We feel good when people like us and count on us. We feel good when we do a service for others.

However, people raised in dysfunctional environments develop an insatiable need for approval and may try to please others as attempts to validate themselves. If we are insecure about our worth, we may become obsessed with making people like us. We may have sex with people when we don't want to. We may loan money to people we don't trust. We may tolerate our friends' bratty children. We may give expensive gifts when we can't afford them.

Sure, people will probably like us better if we are considerate and pleasant. But we can't control people's perceptions of us. Our responsibility is to be kind and polite and still be ourselves.

We don't need others to validate us. We can affirm ourselves. We are intelligent, loving, giving, talented, and beautiful people. The Great Spirit loves us, so do our friends and families. We need to love ourselves.

I please myself and bask in self-validation.

Optimism — *October 6*

Find the good. It's all around you. Find it, showcase it and you'll start believing in it. And so will most of the people who come into contact with you. —JESSE OWENS

光

OPTIMISM HAS GOTTEN A BAD RAP. Some of us think that if we think optimistically we will be duped or disappointed. However, being optimistic doesn't mean being naive. We must realistically evaluate the facts of any situation and admit where we see faults and problems. But we can still have faith that we can solve the problems. There may not be an easy way out. There may not be a happy ending, but we can anticipate a positive outcome.

Optimistic thinking is realistic thinking. Because we change things if we believe that we can. It is only with faith that we can solve problems. Without hope and the ability to expect good, we are lost.

We needn't view the world with rose-colored glasses. When we look around us with faith and love, we will see true radiance and splendor. Reality has its own beauty.

I have faith that good will prevail.

WE ARE ADULTS NOW. IT'S TIME TO LET go of our past. It's time to cut the emotional umbilical cord that ties us to our parents. Sometimes, we hold on to grudges against our parents because of real or perceived hurts.

Our parents are responsible for any abuse—verbal, sexual, physical, mental, spiritual—they perpetrated against us. Abusing children is inexcusable, and it does affect us long past childhood. However, there is a time when we have to claim responsibility for where and how we are. If we were mistreated by our parents, we can heal. We can visit a therapist, participate in a support group, or attend any of the numerous lectures and workshops that are available. We can unlearn inappropriate coping skills we learned as children, and we can discard unhealthy messages.

Perhaps we weren't abused, but our parents were neglectful, overprotective, or unsupportive. We still need to emotionally free ourselves from our parents. We must learn to stand on our own two feet and validate ourselves.

We can sever inappropriate bonds with our parents and replace them with healthy ones. We can establish mature relationships with our parents. It's time to cut the apron springs and enter into full adulthood.

I make peace with my past and own my autonomy.

Be Bold *October 8*

IT CAN BE SCARY TO TRY NEW BEHAVIORS, let go of old ideas. But it's well worth the risk. For when we take the brave, daring step toward self-discovery, we take a step toward true freedom.

If we are afraid, we can imagine ourselves as adventurers of the spirit. Fear didn't stop the first settlers of this land from traveling from Asia to Alaska and spreading across the continent more than twenty thousand years ago. Nor did fear keep Matthew Henson from being one of the first explorers of the North Pole.

Like those great adventurers, we can go on a quest. We can search for knowledge and truth. Today, let's leave doubt behind and take a leap of faith. We'll soar like Bessie Coleman, the first black female aviator, or Guy Bluford, the first black astronaut in space.

I am bold enough to free myself.

You're Not a Quitter — *October 9*

By patience and hard work, we brought order out of chaos, just as will be true of any problem if we stick to it with patience and wisdom and earnest effort. —BOOKER T. WASHINGTON

EVER HAVE ONE OF THOSE DAYS WHEN you just want to pull the covers over your head and stay in bed the rest of your life? You know...the days when the journey gets hard. The way seems unclear. You feel tired, uncertain, or apathetic. You just want to give up.

But you won't give up because you're not a quitter.

We are descended from people who worked from dawn to dusk seven days a week. People—many of whom never learned to read or didn't speak English—who scrimped and saved to send their children to school. People whose faith carried them over mountains of misfortune and across deserts of despair. They didn't quit and we won't quit. We inherited their mettle and determination. We, too, will persevere.

If today is one of those hard days, we can remember that the blood of our ancestors is in us. We can invoke their support. We can ask God to give us strength, as was given to those who went before us. Hang on for one more day. Tomorrow will be better.

I am not a quitter. I persist, and I succeed.

Better Days — *October 10*

You can't get to know better days unless you make it through the night.
—TONY LORRICH

WE'VE MADE IT THROUGH MANY A dark night. Now it's time for better days!

We can make today a better day for ourselves by taking responsibility for our feelings, thoughts, and health. We can stop thinking of ourselves as victims. Nobody can make us feel inferior, bad, or negative unless we let them.

We can make today a better day by being kind to ourselves. We've worked hard during this year, and we deserve to feel good about our accomplishments. We can give ourselves time to relax and recuperate.

We can make today a better day for ourselves by communing with our Higher Power. We can meditate, pray, chant, or just sit quietly. There is nothing like the solace, serenity, and invigoration that comes from spiritual practice.

Let's own our power to make this day joyous, healthful, and fulfilling, and make today a better day.

I have the power to make all my days positive and serene.

Your Inner Child Is Listening *October 11*

THERE ARE MANY THINGS WE WOULDN'T say around children. And we watch our language around our elders out of respect. But how we talk to ourselves!

"How could I be so stupid!" "I'm such a slob." "I look awful." "I could shoot myself for doing that." Can you imagine saying such things to a child or to your best friend? Why is it that we feel obligated to protect others from insults and inappropriate language, but will accept it for ourselves?

Let's be clear: It's *not* OK to abuse ourselves.

We have an inner child, who is impressionable and fragile, who is listening to the messages we give ourselves. Just like any child, we will thrive with gentleness and consideration. Nagging, insulting, or scolding only diminishes us. Let's learn to speak to ourselves with the same care we would a beloved child or a dear friend.

I speak kindly to my inner child.

NOT ONLY CAN WE SURVIVE PERsonal trauma, but we can recover. We can't wash away the memories of being molested, beaten, abandoned, or raped. But we don't have to continue the suffering. We can heal. We also can free ourselves from the stigma of drug, alcohol, food, and sex addictions and lead healthy, fulfilling lives. We won't be cured of an addiction, but the dependency doesn't have to rule our lives.

Today, we can challenge ourselves to heal ourselves. We can go to a Twelve-Step meeting, visit a therapist, talk to a friend, or *whatever it takes* to help ourselves be well. We can give ourselves healing messages of peace, love, and acceptance. Every time we take responsibility for our personal development, we take a step toward healing ourselves.

No matter what our past is like, if we are willing, we can heal.

With each choice and responsible act, I heal.

INTIMACY IS DIFFICULT FOR MANY PEOPLE nowadays. Many of us are suspicious and afraid, which keeps us from the self-disclosure that intimacy requires. While we are more skeptical and wary, we still long to establish close ties with others.

To be intimate with others we have to risk trusting them. We have to risk exposing our deepest thoughts and feelings. We must be willing to let people get to know who we really are. This kind of show and tell may be frightening, especially if we have been betrayed before. But we must get beyond our fear to develop true friendships.

We can give ourselves time to become familiar with other people. We don't have to divulge all our secrets at once. We can wait until we are sure people are trustworthy and slowly share what is in our hearts.

One more note about intimacy: Discretion must be mutual. Let's be careful with the secrets that are shared with us.

I peel back a petal and reveal the bud of my blossoming self.

Treat the Roots *October 14*

OFTEN, WHEN WE HAVE PROBLEMS, WE focus on the surface issues. For example, if we are gaining weight, we go on a diet. If we feel depressed, we try to cheer ourselves up. We do these things without looking at the cause of our problems. In other words, we treat the symptoms. If we want to solve our problems, we must treat the roots.

Unless we get at the root of the problem, we will face it again. We'll regain the weight or depression will set in once again. Like a doctor, we can't prescribe a cure unless we first make an accurate diagnoses.

Not every problem will reach back to childhood issues. There is such a thing as having a bad day or feeling the blues. However, if we battle the same problem time and again, that's a sign that we are suffering from a deeper issue.

Today, let's analyze our problems and determine the true causes. Let's treat the roots.

I dig deep for the origins of my problems and ascertain the correct solutions.

LIFE IS FULL OF DISAPPOINTMENTS—big ones and little ones. It is a major disappointment when we trust someone, and they let us down. It is a minor disappointment when we don't win free tickets during a radio contest. Chances are we can't avoid being disappointed, but there are some disappointments we don't need to suffer.

The family of an American hostage held in the Middle East used to say that they kept their hopes high for their father's release, but their expectations low. We need to hope; hope and faith can carry us through dark, desperate days. However, we also need to be realistic. Like the family of the hostage, we can maintain high hopes *and* realistic expectations.

We can refrain from setting ourselves up to be disappointed by thinking through situations rather than getting carried away by emotions. We can ask ourselves such questions as: Is it wise to trust this person? Is it sensible to expect that to happen?

My expectations are reasonable and wise.

Be Enthusiastic *October 16*

OUR ATTITUDE AFFECTS EVERYTHING we do. If we are confident and upbeat, chances are the activities we participate in will turn out fine. If we are gloomy and insecure, odds are that we will fail. Today, let's do an attitude check and nip self-defeating thoughts in the bud.

If we aren't enthusiastic about our lives, then we can be excited about our opportunities for development. We can be happy about the power we have over our thoughts and beliefs. We don't have to be stuck if we don't want to be. We can experiment, grow, and change. With a positive attitude, we can achieve what we want.

Let's also be aware of how our attitude influences the people we share time with. Like the viruses that go around this time of year, moods are contagious. Rather than infecting others with pessimism, let's give them a shot of enthusiasm. We can encourage and uplift others by sharing our hope and confidence with them.

Enthusiasm is catching.

I brighten my world with a sunny smile and a cheerful disposition.

∴ ∴ ∴ ∴ ∴ ∴ ∴ ∴ ∴ ∴ ∴ ∴ ∴ ∴ ∴ ∴ ∴

Being Whole — *October 17*

IF WE HAVE BEEN ABUSED, WE MAY BLAME ourselves. For example, molested children or battered wives often think it is their fault they are being mistreated. If we think it is our fault, our shame and fear will cause us to reject the parts of us that we think caused our abuse. We'll try to be "good" so we can be loved.

Abuse robs us of the opportunity to get to know ourselves. When we don't know who we really are, we feel incomplete. Like something is missing. Something *is* missing: all those important aspects of ourselves that we've tried to deny because we thought they were dirty, bad, or wrong.

When people are addicted, they also lose a sense of completeness. To hide their addiction, they lie and pretend to be something they're not.

When we recover from childhood abuse or addictions, we find the parts of ourselves we were cut off from. We embrace the parts of ourselves we were taught to hate or hide. We incorporate our feelings. We determine our values. We put together the pieces of the puzzle that make up ourselves. If we feel fractured and confused, we can feel whole again. We can solve the mysteries of our past.

I thank my Higher Power for restoring me to wholeness.

All things are connected. Whatever befalls the earth befalls the children of the earth. —CHIEF SEATTLE

POLLUTION, OVERPOPULATION, AND DEforestation are just some of the hazards to our planet and to its inhabitants.

We would benefit by becoming more environmentally aware. For example, many landfills, chemical plants, and nuclear waste dumps are located in our neighborhoods. We can determine if they are detrimental to our land, water, and air and fight to get them cleaned up.

We also can become more conscious of how our actions affect the world and can change our personal habits. We can use public transportation, carpool, ride bikes, or walk. We can recycle newspapers, bottles, and cans. We can support food producers who don't use chemicals, pesticides, or steroids.

We are the children of Mother Earth and Father Sky. We have a duty to protect that which has given birth to us, that which is our home.

I treat my "mother" with love and respect.

Giving *October 19*

IT IS MARVELOUS TO GIVE TO OTHERS. However, we must be sure that our generosity is beneficial for all concerned.

Some of us give, give, give until we give ourselves away. If we are so busy giving that we don't allow ourselves to receive or we don't give to ourselves, pretty soon we'll have nothing to offer. We can't give what we don't have.

Sometimes we give because we think we are being generous, but we are really being manipulative. We give with strings attached; we want something back. We want people to like us, approve of us, feel sorry for us, feel indebted to us. This type of manipulation causes resentment and disappointment. Our friends may end up resenting our gifts and favors, and we may be offended when we don't receive anything in return.

We can distinguish healthy giving by how it makes us feel. If we feel resentful or disappointed about the recipient's response, perhaps we have hidden motives for our gifts. If we feel exhausted and used, perhaps we are caught up in martyrdom and need to stop playing the victim. Our inner guides will tell us how to give well when we listen.

I give wholeheartedly and honestly as much as it feels good for me to give.

KNOWING HOW TO RECEIVE GRACIOUSLY is just as important as knowing how to give. Well-adjusted people allow for give and take in relationships.

If we've been doing all the giving, today, let's allow ourselves to receive. We need love, support, praise, and attention from people. We need their warm words and snuggly hugs. We need guidance, favors, and assistance. There is no shame in being the recipient every now and then. It is OK for us to let others give to us.

If you've been on the giving end of the spectrum, today it will be better to receive. Give yourself a gift today and allow yourself to receive from others. You deserve it.

I gratefully accept kindness and assistance from the people who love me.

PEOPLE ARE GROWING COLDER, MORE immune to violence and despair. We step over people lying in the streets. We turn the channel when pleas to help starving children come on the screen. We watch movies where most of the characters are shot, stabbed, or bombed.

Think of how different the world would be if everyone knew they were loved. Society's problems seem overwhelming, but we *can* make a difference. We can heal the world with love. We can start with those around us—we can tell our families and friends how much we love them. We can send notes and gifts anonymously. We can do favors without being asked. We can brush the snow off our spouse's car. We can spend an extra half an hour on bath-and-bedtime playing with the kids. We can bake a fresh batch of chocolate chip cookies and share them with a neighbor. We can help a co-worker finish a project.

We also can reach out to people we don't know. People who desperately need to know they matter. Homeless people, prisoners, gang members, teenage mothers, runaways, battered women and children, junkies—people who are lost and have given up hope.

I call on the love that has made a difference in my life to help others.

∵ ∵ ∵ ∵ ∵ ∵ ∵ ∵ ∵ ∵ ∵ ∵ ∵ ∵ ∵ ∵ ∵

Wise Up *October 22*

THE WORLD IS A SCHOOL. PEOPLE, animals, trees, rivers, and stars are our teachers. Like our ancestors, we can learn as much from a butterfly or bee as we can from a fellow traveler. Unlike many of our ancestors, we also have the ability to receive a formal education. But, even if we can't afford to go to college or don't enjoy school, we still need to be educated.

We may believe in education to further our careers, but our jobs aren't the only aspects of our life that will benefit from a well-rounded education. We need information to make intelligent decisions about everything in our lives. We need to wise up.

We need knowledge to keep up with all the changes and protect ourselves from unscrupulous people. Unfortunately, some people want to take advantage of our ignorance and naïveté.

Today, let's educate ourselves. Let's take a class. Let's read newspapers, books, and magazines. Let's ask questions and get involved with issues. Let's learn about the environment, politics, sociology, philosophy, psychology, or any other discipline that interests us. An education opens the door to a world of opportunity. All we have to do is turn the key.

I wisely take advantage of my opportunities for enlightenment.

Have a Plan *October 23*

AS WE SET OFF ON OUR JOURNEY through life, it helps if we have a map. We need direction to show us the way. As we mature, we head for new territory like the exodusters did when they left the south to build a new life on the plains. We must develop a plan to follow so that all our steps lead us to our desired destination. We wouldn't leave for a cross-country trip without noting the best route to take; let's not go through life without a plan.

A life plan can help us meet our goals. We can begin by deciding long-term goals. Where do we want to be five, ten, or twenty years from now? We can create short-term plans that will help us build toward our long-term goals. What can we do this year to help us do what we want to do next year? Next year's plan will help us move to the next.

We can build our goals one step at a time. Have a plan, then execute it.

I prudently chart my course through life.

Everyday Victories — *October 24*

Set your own goals for success, the only one to blame for failure is yourself. —ALEX REYES

MANY PEOPLE THINK OF SUCCESS IN terms of money, fame, security, and power. There's nothing wrong with wanting to achieve superstar status in business, the arts, sports, or education. However, celebrity and wealth aren't the only measures of success.

We can consider ourselves successful when we respect and value ourselves and our brothers and sisters, know ourselves and share what we know with others, and hold on to our ambition, faith, and confidence no matter what adversities we face.

Today, let's stretch our idea of success to include personal fulfillment and sharing. Let's celebrate "everyday victories," like when we assert ourselves, readily admit an error, or tell the truth. Let's also encourage our loved ones to enjoy the success of living to their highest potential.

I am a success at life!

Mission Statement *October 25*

I suppose I am kept here because something remains for me to do; I suppose I am yet to help break the chain.

—SOJOURNER TRUTH

MOST BUSINESSES HAVE A MISSION statement that explains how they operate and what goals they plan to achieve. This statement creates a vision for all employees and lets customers know what to expect from the company.

Individuals, too, can create mission statements. We can develop a personal policy that declares our purpose, sets goals, and creates expectations.

What is your mission? Write it down. Keep it in your desk, wallet, or taped to your bathroom mirror. Look at it periodically to remind yourself of your purpose. Use it to make decisions about what you are doing. If an activity meets the requirements of your mission statement, do it. If it does not, don't do it.

I know my mission and act accordingly.

Scapegoats *October 26*

RACISTS BLAME PEOPLE OF COLOR FOR many of this nation's problems. They either don't understand the complex origins of economic and social problems or can't accept the truth. They make people of color the scapegoat for the problems.

Families also create scapegoats. For example, rather than admitting the problem is Dad's drinking, the family decides everything would be fine if Junior just got good grades in school. Or a man might say he would stop beating his wife if his boss would lighten up on him. A woman might think she wouldn't cheat on her husband if she wasn't alone so much.

Mature adults don't have scapegoats. Nor do they play the role of the scapegoat for others.

I accept complete responsibility for myself and my life. If there is a problem, I use my energy to find a solution, rather than to lay blame.

THERE ARE MANY GOOD REASONS TO exercise. Statistics show that people who exercise have lower rates of disease such as cancer and arthritis. Exercise enthusiasts also claim more freedom of movement well into old age.

Physical exertion makes us healthier mentally and physically. When we work out, our brains release endorphins that make us feel better and increase the supply of glucose in the brain. Mounting evidence suggests being physically fit can make us more mentally and emotionally fit.

Today, let's take a walk, go skating, jump rope, join an aerobics class, lift weights, play basketball, go swimming, learn karate. We also can build more activity into our lives by riding our bikes, walking to work, and taking the stairs instead of the elevator.

Bring back a sense of play and movement to your life. Your body and your mind will thank you.

I am active, fit, and healthy.

Share the Credit *October 28*

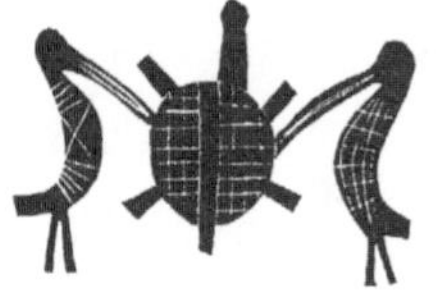

SOMETIMES IT'S DIFFICULT TO GIVE praise to others for the assistance they've given us. We may prefer to think that we accomplished our goals on our own. We may perceive admitting that we learned from others as a sign of failure.

It is not a fault to need help from others. It is a sign of strength and intelligence when we turn to others for assistance. It is a sign of generosity and confidence when we can tell others how much they have helped us.

Let's share the credit with those who deserve it. Like the actors at the Academy Awards, we can take time to thank all the people who made our success possible. The teachers who recognized our creativity, the mentors who challenged us to reach beyond our self-imposed limitations, the parents or grandparents who taught us how to love, the lovers who gave us a shoulder to cry on, and the co-worker who pitched in on a big project share the credit for who we are today. Let's tell them.

We can acknowledge our efforts *and* the assistance of others. We won't miss out on praise by sharing it with others. There is enough praise and credit for us all.

I happily acknowledge the contributions others have made to my success.

Fear *October 29*

He who fears is literally delivered to destruction.

—HOWARD THURMAN

INDEED, HE WHO FEARS ACTUALLY CAUSES his own destruction. Fear saps our energies and our ability to act in our own best interests. Trying to find solutions to our problems from a mind-set of fear doesn't work. The only way we can better ourselves is through love and faith.

Being afraid is like turning our backs on ourselves and on God. Fear is faithlessness, because if we believed, what would we have to fear? If we believed we could handle any situation, what could scare us? If we believed that we have the love and guidance of our Higher Power, what could scare us? If we believed that we can learn and grow from any event, what could scare us?

We don't have to be afraid. We can believe. We can have faith in the universe and confidence in ourselves. We can remember a tragedy or a time of great anguish and concern and remind ourselves that we survived. We are here and we are all right. No matter what happens, we are all right because we always have God's love. Our faith is what will deliver us from the devastation of fear.

My faith is stronger than fear.

Support Groups *October 30*

Alas, the journey of life is beset with thorns to those who have to travel it alone. —ALEXANDRE DUMAS

IF WE ARE FORTUNATE, WE HAVE STRONG, healthy relationships with family members and/or friends. However, some of us aren't so lucky. Some of us may move frequently, which makes it hard to establish close ties. Some of us may come from dysfunctional families and have no desire to bond with relatives. We all need connection with someone.

A support group can give us comfort by understanding exactly how we feel. People with illnesses and addictions especially benefit from interactions with people who share the same experiences. There are also support groups for single parents, divorced people, grieving people, and just about any other category you can imagine. If we are concerned about sharing our experiences with strangers, rest assured that participants in these groups don't stay strangers for long.

Being able to share our worries, fears, hopes, joys, and triumphs with people who understand, care, and empathize is very healing. Whether it's family, friends, or "strangers," we all need a support group. We don't have to travel the journey of life alone.

I deserve the love and support of friends.

Skeletons in the Closet *October 31*

ONE TRAIT OF DYSFUNCTIONAL families is that they keep secrets from each other and from people outside the family. Family secrets range in severity from mother telling daughter "Don't tell your father how much we spent at the mall" to an incestuous parent telling a child "Don't tell anybody what we do at night."

Asking a child to collude against a parent or sibling is abusive. It puts an unfair burden on a child to ask him to keep a secret from his friends, parents, or siblings, especially a secret about how he feels or is being treated. It's difficult to keep secrets from children; they are very perceptive. They may not know what is going on, but they will know something is wrong. While children don't need to know—and may not be able to understand—what goes on in the parents' marriage, it is better to explain disturbing situations to them. By being honest, we can validate children's feelings and teach them to trust their instincts.

We are only as sick as our secrets. Today, let's vanquish fears that cause us to hide our thoughts and feelings. We don't have to hide anymore. The only time skeletons belong in closets is on Halloween.

I make healthy choices about what to share and what to keep private.

Materialism *November 1*

It was our belief that the love of possessions is a weakness to be overcome. —OHIYESA (CHARLES ALEXANDER EASTMAN)

AMERICAN SOCIETY IS OBSESSED with wealth. We all say "money doesn't buy happiness," but how many of us spend more time in shopping malls than libraries? How many of us give *things* to our loved ones instead of the attention and caring they truly need? How many of us have been willing to sell our souls for material goods?

We get preoccupied with attaining wealth and amassing more and more things. The more stuff we have, the more stuff we think we need. Let's be clear about the difference between wants and needs. We need sufficient shelter, transportation, and adequate clothing. But most of us do not need a three-story, five-bathroom, three-car-garage house. We do not need luxury cars and designer wardrobes. These are things we want.

It's not wrong to want fine things, but we should do so with knowledge that these things will not bring us happiness. Only love of others, God, and self and engaging in meaningful activities brings the deep personal satisfaction that we want *and* need.

I turn to healthy relationships and communing with the Creator—not things—for love and happiness.

AS LONG AS WE ARE MENTALLY ENslaved, we'll never be free. Psychological freedom is the most powerful weapon against adversity. Because when our minds are free, we can think for ourselves. We can achieve any goal.

Our physical freedom has been hard-won, so is psychological freedom. We must continue to fight for our freedom. We must question the rules and values we live with.

No matter what the Declaration of Independence says, unless our minds are free, we are still slaves. Whether the master is an overseer or a false belief, we are still slaves.

Today, let's free our minds and our spirits from negative thinking, stereotypical ideas, and bad habits.

I am free in every sense of the word.

"DON'T WORRY, BE HAPPY" SOUNDS pretty frivolous to people who have a history of abuse or discrimination. "Of course we're worried! Look at the state of the world," we think. We may believe that people who aren't worried are crazy.

But the truth is worrying doesn't help. Worrying doesn't fix anything. Worrying is not the answer. Unless worrying causes us to act, it actually hampers our ability to find constructive solutions to our problems.

Today, we can relax our vigilance. The world will manage without our control. Let's not sweat the small stuff and save our energy for the things that *can* benefit from our attention.

Relax. Chill out. Be easy. Be well. Think. Then act. See how much more effective you are?

I am relaxed and centered.

Saying Good-bye   *November 4*

THE BEGINNINGS OF FRIENDSHIPS and romances are always more fun than the endings. However, sometimes we have to say good-bye.

Divorce is a trauma that takes a long time for people to get over. A couple goes into a marriage with high hopes for building a life together. It's never easy to see those dreams shattered. Divorce that is not mutually agreed upon is especially hard, and when children are involved, it's devastating.

The death of a friend, relative, or lover can be overwhelmingly painful. It's hard to accept that the person is gone forever.

It's perfectly natural to feel sad and lonely when we must say good-bye. We can lessen the pain by accepting our feelings. We can lessen the pain by changing our perceptions of good-byes. In relationships, stories, goals, and in life, endings are just as important as beginnings. Good-byes and hellos are part of the same cycle.

Endings make room for beginnings.

Saying good-bye to one thing is part of saying hello to another.

No Whining — *November 5*

It is of no use for us to sit with our hands folded, hanging our heads like bulrushes, lamenting our wretched condition; but let us make a mighty effort, and arise; and if no one will promote or respect us, let us promote and respect ourselves.

—MRS. MARIA W. STEWART

WOE IS ME. LIFE STINKS. AIN'T I PITIful?... Yuck! What pathetic messages to give ourselves! Yet, this is what we do when we whine. The only good thing about whining is that it doesn't waste any brain power.

If we were using our brains, we would know that whining is a complete waste of energy, time, and tears. The power we waste on whining could be used for changing whatever we are unhappy with. Self-pity is a destructive cycle. Whining only leads to more whining.

Today, no pouting, sulking, moping, complaining, or criticizing is allowed—no matter what is going on in our lives. We don't have to "grin and bear it." But if something is wrong, let's do something about it.

Let's stop throwing ourselves pity parties and start celebrating our power to act.

I have no complaints. All is well in my world.

Dealing with Conflict *November 6*

CONFLICTS ARE A PART OF LIFE. We can have disputes with friends, family members, employees, neighbors, waiters, or anybody with whom we interact. Conflicts can't be avoided, but we can learn to handle them better.

The first thing we can do is not take it personally if someone confronts us about our behavior. We can listen to the person, and if they have a point, we can apologize about our behavior and make amends. If we disagree with their charges, we can explain our behavior to clarify why we do what we do and defend ourselves. Open discussions about what people think and feel about how we treat them are healthy.

We also need not be afraid of talking to others about issues we may have. It is our right to tell others what we like and don't like about how they treat us. Getting things out on the table is good for relationships. When we communicate in this manner, we give others a chance to learn more about us and explain if we have misinterpreted something they said or did.

If handled appropriately, conflicts can clear the air and bring people closer together.

I do not fear confrontation. Conflicts are healthy, natural, and normal.

Listening *November 7*

TALK, TALK, TALK, TALK, TALK. MOST people haven't learned the art of conversation. They interrupt, change the subject, and just don't listen. Being fully engaged in conversations—even when they aren't speaking—is a characteristic of good communicators. It's called active listening.

In active listening, the listener tries to feel what the speaker is feeling, tries to understand what the speaker is thinking. Instead of assuming "I know just what you mean," the active listener asks "If I understand you, you mean…" The speaker has a chance to clarify herself and the listener has a chance to make sure she comprehends the speaker's point. Active listening creates more interesting, meaningful dialogues between folks.

The active listener also keeps his mouth shut until it is clear the speaker has finished speaking. During conversations, silence is definitely a virtue. We have much to learn from people, but we are often so busy preparing a witty response that we don't hear the lessons. It's difficult to pay complete attention to others, especially when the conversation seems mundane. However, we never know what underlying message people are trying to give us unless we listen closely.

Instead of talking at people, I listen to them.

A HYPOCRITE IS A PERSON WHO SAYS one thing and does another. A person who professes to believe in a principle, but whose actions demonstrate something else. A fake. A fraud. A phony.

Today, let's ask ourselves if *we* are walking our talk. Do we claim to be proud of our heritage, yet disparage our brothers and sisters? Do we say we want to be treated with respect, yet disrespect ourselves? Do we call ourselves religious, yet act cruelly or unethically?

When we say one thing and do another, it is confusing. People get mixed signals about how to treat us. And we don't send a clear indication to ourselves about what we want and need.

Actions speak louder than words. Let's make sure our actions are conveying the same message that our words do. Let's make sure that we aren't giving ourselves and others double messages.

I practice what I preach.

Harmony *November 9*

There is an essential harmony in all existence, and the life of every living thing shares in it. —HOWARD THURMAN

TO BE IN HARMONY IS TO LIVE IN ACcord with nature and the universe. Our ancestors knew well the benefits of living in harmony. Let's tap into the harmonic forces in the universe to solve the problems in our community. Gang wars, racism, sexism, and political infighting are evidence of people who are not in harmony with each other or themselves.

We must be in harmony with our inner selves. If we aren't doing what deep down inside we know to be best for us, there will be conflict. We will feel uncomfortable and ashamed and suffer from dis-ease.

We also need to peacefully coexist with our brethren—complimenting each other and working together. World harmony begins with inner harmony.

I live in harmony with all living things.

食 OUR PEOPLE HAVE BEEN BLESSED WITH riches of the spirit. Those of us whose ancestors broke their backs building this country inherited a wealth of strength and vitality. Those of us who came to this country to escape dictatorships, police states, poverty, and hunger were graced with an abundance of courage and determination.

America offers a smorgasbord of opportunities that other countries do not. Our people haven't always been invited to the table to share the feast. But now we can pull up a chair. We don't have to wait for the government or anybody else to make room for us. It's time to sit at the table we helped build. It's time to partake of the meal we helped cook.

Responsibilities come with joining the banquet. We must be ready to serve all our brothers and sisters at the table; there is no room for selfishness. We must be prepared to make a place for the next person who decides to join the party. We also must focus on the contributions we can make to replace the goodies we have enjoyed. We have a duty to make sure the feast continues for the next generation.

I am a welcome guest at the banquet of life. I accept my place at the table.

Our Legacy *November 11*

WE HAVE A RICH INHERITANCE OF spirituality, wisdom, courage, and fortitude. Today, let's ask ourselves what type of example are we setting for future generations? What will we leave behind? What will be our legacy to our children and the earth?

Let's take stock of our lives to ensure we are creating a healthy path for others to follow. We want to give our children a paradigm that doesn't forfeit values for vanity or trade people for profit. We want to leave behind a foundation for our children to build on that is based on integrity and love. We want to give them a ladder so they can climb to the heights of happiness. We want to save enough resources so our successors will have the materials they will need to provide for their children.

Let's honor the gifts we have received from our ancestors by giving to our descendants.

I build a legacy I will be proud to leave behind.

Just for Today *November 12*

"JUST FOR TODAY" IS A TWELVE-STEP PROgram maxim that helps people face some of the major changes necessary for recovery. Making changes just for today isn't as overwhelming as thinking about making permanent changes. If something is difficult, it's easier for people to bear it just for today. This philosophy also reassures people and encourages experimenting with unorthodox behaviors. If we don't like the results, we can try something different.

Just for today we can take inventory of our actions and accept responsibility for our choices. Just for today we can make amends to ourselves and treat ourselves with kindness. Just for today we can let go of controlling behaviors and trust that all will be well. We make gains in our growth by trying new ideas one day at a time.

I live just for this day, enjoying all that it has to offer and giving all that I can.

Internalized Racism *November 13*

If it seems that your color is the reason,…it's because you've been deliberately beaten down by agents of a greedy system until you swallowed the garbage. —GLORIA YAMATO

INTERNALIZED RACISM IS TAKING THE LIES and abuse that have been perpetrated against us and perpetrating them against ourselves. It's when we subconsciously—and sometimes consciously—distrust a person of color in authority, believing they couldn't be competent. It's when we are uncomfortable in the environments of our cultures, turning up our noses at the food, language, and music. Simply put, it's when we are ashamed of who we are and where we come from.

When we discount, disrespect, and disavow ourselves, we do more damage to our spirits than any racist ever could. We stifle our creativity, ignore our health, and forget our choices. And, worse yet, we pass these shaming messages on to the next generation.

It's time to end this cycle of self-abuse. We can start by learning the truth about our ancestry: Our respective histories and cultures are incredibly rich—filled with bravery, genius, ingenuity, and spirituality. Next we can learn the truth about ourselves.

I end the cycle of self-abuse by treating myself with kindness.

Reasonable Expectations *November 14*

REASONABLE EXPECTATIONS ALLOW us to set goals and make contracts with people. Unreasonable expectations set us up to be disappointed and frustrated. How can we tell the difference?

The best indicator of future behavior is past performance. Therefore, we can't realistically expect liars to be honest, latecomers to be on time, adulterers to be loyal, or people who never call us to suddenly pick up the phone. Of course, it is possible for people to change, and we can always hope for their growth, but it's unwise to count on it.

It is reasonable to require decent, respectful behavior from our friends and family. If people don't exhibit the behavior and principles we value, we can choose not to associate with them. However, it is irrational to expect even the most wonderful friend to be 100 percent honest or 100 percent supportive. Everybody has an off day.

Today, let's be fair to others and to ourselves and operate with realistic expectations.

I protect myself from disappointment and cut others some slack by having reasonable expectations.

Guardian Angels *November 15*

MANY NATIVE AMERICAN, LATINO, Asian, and African cultures believe their ancestors' spirits guide and protect them.

We, too, can believe in spirits that watch out for us. Our guardian angels may be loved ones who have entered the spirit world, or they can be the friends and neighbors who help us. Our sponsors, confidants, mates, and elders were sent from the heavens to teach us. Spirits tell us long-forgotten secrets about the ways of nature, love, and God. Let's listen to them, for they know the way. Let's be grateful for the angels in our lives that direct us and keep us from harm. Let's tell our friends how much we appreciate their love and support.

I open my mind to the wisdom and comfort provided by my guardian angels.

Now, as we dare to take responsibility for our own future as individuals and peoples, as we give up the fantasy that presidents or the best charismatic leaders can solve the most basic problems of our society, the moment of great possibility opens before us.

—VINCENT HARDING

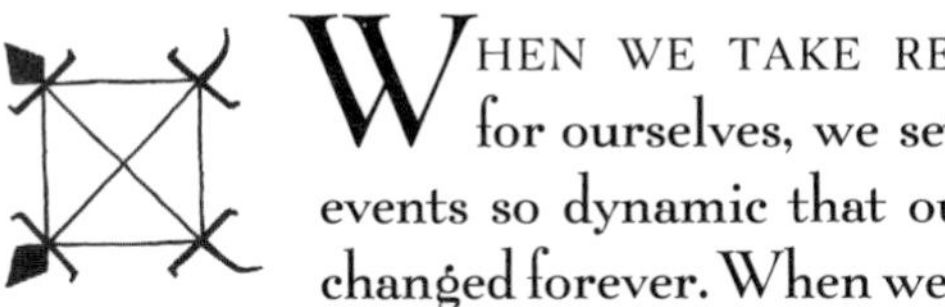

WHEN WE TAKE RESPONSIBILITY for ourselves, we set off a chain of events so dynamic that our lives will be changed forever. When we accept responsibility for ourselves, we assume the power to fix whatever is broken, to right whatever is wrong. We also gain the right to claim praise for whatever is right in our lives.

It is not the responsibility of politicians, community leaders, preachers, priests, chiefs, spouses, or anybody else to save us. We must take care of ourselves.

I accept responsibility for my life with gratitude for the possibilities afforded me.

Self-Fulfilling Prophecy *November 17*

WE MAY NOT BE ABLE TO PREDICT SPEcifics about our future nor will ourselves to win the lottery, but what we believe, comes true.

Our beliefs about ourselves determine where we go and what we will achieve in life; they are self-fulfilling prophecies. If we expect to prosper, we will. If we expect to be defeated by racism, sexism, or poverty, we will be.

The key to our health, happiness, and success is in our minds. Let's believe in the glorious future the universe has in store for us. By believing, we will create it.

Today, I foresee success.

'TIS THE SEASON TO BE JOLLY...RIGHT? for many of us, this time of year is full of happiness, togetherness, and giving. But for some, Thanksgiving, Hanukkah, Christmas, and Kwanza can feel lonely and meaningless.

Those of us who dread the holidays can think of ways to make them easier on ourselves. During this holiday season, we can give ourselves permission to take care of ourselves.

We can say no to some invitations. We can shop in catalogs, give gift certificates, or buy fewer gifts.

If the holidays bring melancholy memories of departed loved ones, we can acknowledge our grief. We can allow ourselves to cry and be sad.

If we dread spending time with dysfunctional relatives, we can avoid them or set boundaries. We have the right to choose who we spend time with.

Choose what makes you feel good this holiday season. Spend time with friends who support and love you. Give gifts that have meaning for you. You might be able to lift your depression by helping those in need. People in shelters and hospices would be grateful to have someone to talk to for an hour or two.

I plan how I want to spend this holiday season and acknowledge my right to celebrate (or not celebrate) however I choose.

On the Fence *November 19*

SOMETIMES WE ARE AFRAID TO MAKE A decision, so we straddle the fence trying to have it both ways. But we can't. We have to choose.

Though it may feel safe, sitting on the fence is actually a stressful place to be. If we recoil from taking action, we become more conflicted and confused. The very thing we fear—making a decision—is the only thing that will end our anxiety.

Today, let's get off the fence. We don't have to be afraid. We have what it takes to make the right decisions for us. We know in our hearts what we need and what we want. All we have to do is tap into our intuitive selves and mine the wisdom that is in the deepest parts of our souls.

I climb down from my perch and take a stand.

How We Look *November 20*

Don't be afraid to show your colors and to own them.

—WILLIAM WELLS BROWN

IT SEEMS TO BE HUMAN NATURE TO JUDGE one person in comparison with another. The danger lies in using a dysfunctional standard. Many people in this country consider European features as the norm to measure beauty against. Therefore, many people of color are ashamed of their facial features and hair texture because they think they don't measure up. What a shame.

But it doesn't have to be this way. Each and every one of us can let go of racist concepts of beauty and learn to see the beauty of *all* people. We can learn to see the beauty in ourselves. Today and every day, we have permission to carry our heads high. No matter how your eyes are shaped, how large or small your nose is, how straight or curly your hair, how wide or narrow your hips, you are beautiful.

I am grateful to my Higher Power for the beauty that is within me.

You Are Changing *November 21*

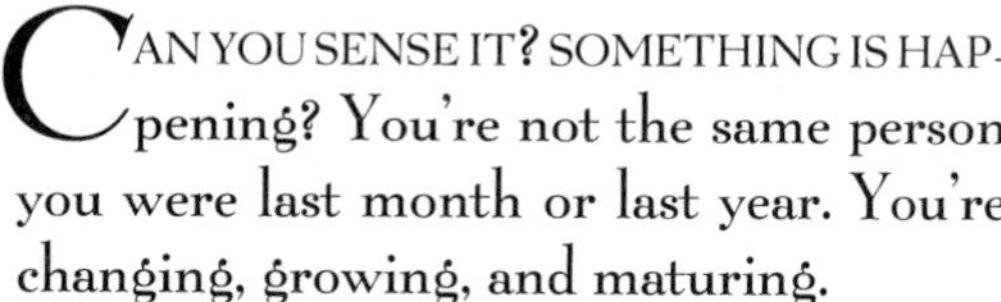

CAN YOU SENSE IT? SOMETHING IS HAPPENING? You're not the same person you were last month or last year. You're changing, growing, and maturing.

When we commit ourselves to healthy lifestyles and take charge of our choices, we get better. We grow stronger, wiser, more confident, and more serene. We can take inventory of all the positive changes we have made in our lives. We can thank our Creator for giving us the freedom to choose to improve ourselves. We can be proud of ourselves for owning our power of choice.

Today, let's take the evidence of all the wonderful things that are happening to us and use it to dedicate ourselves even further.

Each day I take a step toward accepting all that I am and becoming all that I want to be.

Fear of Death *November 22*

THOUGH WE DON'T LIKE TO THINK about it, we are all going to die. It's difficult to comprehend that one day we won't be here. Is there a heaven? Will we be back again? No one knows for certain what happens on the other side. What we do know is that people who take full advantage of their lives die with the least regrets. It's a bit of a paradox, but the people who are most afraid of dying are the people who haven't fully lived. People who have enjoyed their lives die in peace, no matter how old they are.

The lesson is that whether we are twenty-five or eighty-five we should face the reality that our lives (at least as we know them) will cease. We don't have to be morbid or preoccupied with death, but we can let our awareness of death teach us to appreciate life.

We don't know when our time will end. So let's make each day count. Being conscious of death can help us be conscious of life. We can reflect on death, not to frighten ourselves, but to prod ourselves to act.

I am ever aware of the sacredness of each breath.

What Goes Around — *November 23*

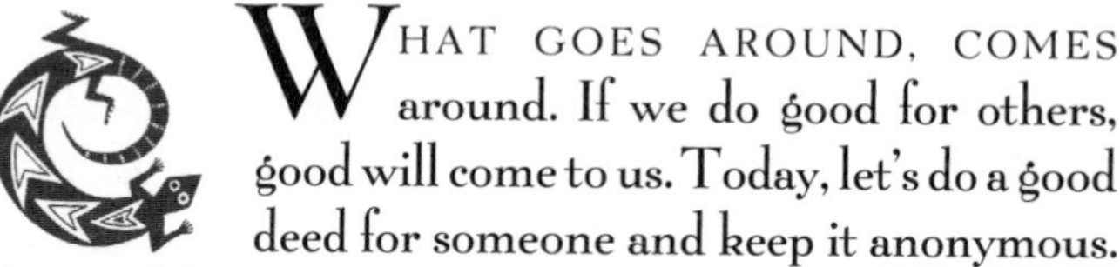

WHAT GOES AROUND, COMES around. If we do good for others, good will come to us. Today, let's do a good deed for someone and keep it anonymous. We can deliver a newspaper to our neighbor's home or put money in a stranger's parking meter.

Or we can do a favor for someone without expecting anything in return. Let's do it for the pure pleasure of knowing that we've helped another person. We can baby-sit for a friend without planning to deliver our kids the next day. We can wash the dishes, even though it is our roommate's turn. We can give the right-of-way to other drivers.

We don't have to worry about how we will be rewarded for our good deed. What we put out to the universe comes back to us in spades.

I do good deeds, knowing that when I give to others I give to myself.

Humility *November 24*

Of course it was not I who cured. It was the power from the outer world, and the visions and ceremonies had only made me like a hole through which the power could come to the two-leggeds. If I thought I was doing it myself, the hole would close up and no power could come through. —BLACK ELK

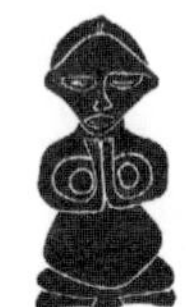

MANY OF US MAY THINK OF HUMILITY as meaning being bashful, nonassertive, or even submissive. This is not true. The word humble comes from the Greek and Latin words for earth, hence the saying "down to earth." When we are humble, we may be down to earth, but we are in a position to reach the stars.

When we are humble, we allow God to work through us, to inspire and guide us. When we are humble, we realize that it's OK to need help from our brothers and sisters.

When we open ourselves to direction from God and support from others, we have access to infinitely more power than we could ever have on our own. We become stronger, more effective people.

I humbly acknowledge the divine power working through me.

Gratitude *November 25*

THIS IS THE TIME OF YEAR (PARticularly on Thanksgiving Day) that people start counting their blessings. We thank God for our health, homes, and families. We say prayers and give gifts to express our gratitude for all we have received. It is important to voice our thankfulness to our Higher Power and to our loved ones.

We also can show our gratitude by sharing our blessings with others. If we have money, we can contribute to charity or take in foster children or adopt a child. If we have extra time, we can volunteer to help clean up the environment, teach people to read, comfort people who are sick, or counsel people who need assistance. Whatever the Great Spirit has blessed us with, we can bestow upon others.

I have an attitude of gratitude and share my good fortunes with others.

Hard Times — *November 26*

I've not forgotten the song of those dark years, hambre del alma, *the song of the starved soul. But neither have I forgotten the joyous* canto hondo, *the deep song, the words of which come back to us when we do the work of soulful reclamation.*

—CLARISSA PINKOLA ESTÉS

"LIFE IS SUFFERING" IS ONE OF THE four noble truths of Buddhism. This does not mean that we are meant to suffer. It means that once we realize that there will be pain in life—and facing that pain requires discipline and responsibility—we can ease our own suffering. Once we accept this truth, we can reclaim the words to the "*canto hondo.*"

The journey toward maturity will bring pain, which is meant to teach us. Hard times are part of life, but not the only part. We are also meant to rejoice, have fun, and find peace. Just because we sing the blues today, doesn't mean tomorrow won't be better. We may sing the "*hambre del alma,*" but if we commit ourselves to recovery, it won't be the only song we sing.

The lessons I learn today help me sing a song of joy tomorrow.

FRIENDS ARE ONE OF OUR GREATEST gifts. Let's devote today to developing our friendships. We can tell our close friends how grateful we are for their friendship. We can send a little gift "just because" or write a cheery note just to say "I'm thinking of you." Friends need to hear "I love you" just as much as sweethearts and relatives do.

We can spend some time becoming more familiar with our acquaintances. We can ask the person who works in our building to join us for lunch. We can take a cup of cocoa to the neighbor shoveling the sidewalk. With time and attention, these casual relationships may build to more intimate friendships.

We also can just plain be more friendly and develop a cordial attitude. We can introduce ourselves to the cashiers at our grocery stores and say hello to the mail carrier. If you want to have a friend, be a friend.

I am blessed with many loving friends.

Control *November 28*

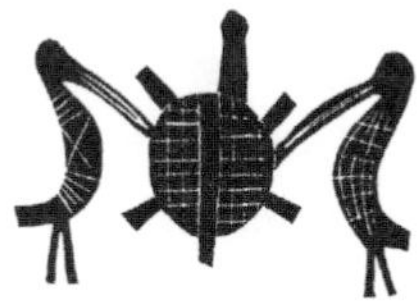

IT IS OUR RESPONSIBILITY TO OVERsee our children. They need supervision, discipline, and guidance to prepare them for adulthood. Though children should be allowed to make some of their own decisions, they aren't emotionally or mentally equipped to fully manage their own lives.

Grown-ups, on the other hand, should take complete responsibility for handling their affairs. We may know people we wish we could control; people who underestimate, disrespect, or devalue themselves. Because we love them, we want to be able to force them to treat themselves better. While in extreme cases—when someone is suicidal, mentally ill, or chronically addicted—we can intervene to help, in most instances all we can do is give counsel and support.

Trying to control people doesn't work. Those we try to dominate dislike us...and *do what they want anyway.*

We can't control others, but we can control what we allow in our lives. We can choose healthy, self-respecting people for friends and mates. We can set boundaries for what we feel is appropriate behavior.

Today, if we are uncertain about what we can control and what we can't, we can say the Serenity Prayer. Clarity will come.

I allow others to run their own lives.

Listening to Ourselves — *November 29*

You have to decide that what other people think of you and what you've been taught is not important and that you are going to evaluate things for yourself and see if they make sense.

—DIANE NASH

FROM THE MOMENT WE COME INTO THIS world we are learning. We learn from our parents, siblings, teachers, friends, the media, religion—from society in general. Some of what we learn is very valuable. But some of our lessons are misleading. Some are downright lies.

The most important lesson we need to learn is to listen to our hearts, the inner voice that tells us what is true and right for us. Our ancestors knew this. Our elders knew that people must find their own way in this world...walk their own path. We might even remember grandmothers and grandfathers who told us to believe in God and ourselves and ignore the rest. Think back: what did we learn as children? What lessons are we living by that we want to keep? What rules are we living by that don't work for us anymore?

We have the power to live our lives as we see fit. The answers that we seek are inside ourselves. All we have to do is listen.

I have the answers inside myself.

The "Lost" Child — November 30

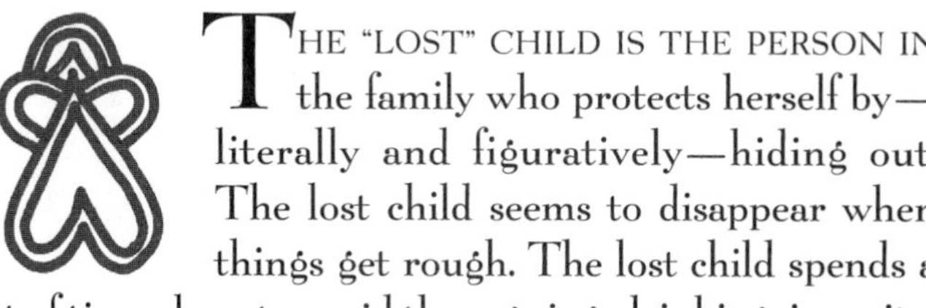

THE "LOST" CHILD IS THE PERSON IN the family who protects herself by—literally and figuratively—hiding out. The lost child seems to disappear when things get rough. The lost child spends a lot of time alone to avoid the arguing, drinking, insanity, or violence. Lost children also try to escape the chaos around them by burying their heads in books, movies, or lively fantasies. Lost children are so good at playing invisible that other family members often "forget" them. Lost children also are adept at not calling attention to themselves by being well-behaved.

For those of us who were the lost children in our families, it's time to come out. It's time to find ourselves. We have much to offer that we can't give if we sit quietly while the world passes us by. We are strong adults who can defend ourselves. We can speak our minds and set healthy boundaries to protect ourselves. We don't have to be invisible anymore. We don't have to be afraid anymore.

I step out of the shadows and claim my right to be seen and heard. I show myself without fear.

Self-Reliance — *December 1*

Action, self-reliance, the vision of self and the future have been the only means by which the oppressed have seen and realized the light of their own freedom. —MARCUS GARVEY

WE DESERVE FAIR AND EQUAL TREATMENT from others, though we may not always receive it. However, blaming others for our status gets us nowhere. Racist and sexist beliefs *do* dominate American culture and can be devastating. But we can't let those beliefs or anything else stop us from achieving our goals.

The only way to realize our dreams is by taking personal responsibility for where we are and committing ourselves to moving forward.

It can be disheartening to realize that some people will judge us by the color of our skin, rather than our actions, skills, and character. It may be helpful to think about the courage, perseverance, and resilience of the people who have gone before us: Wilma Mankiller, Samuel Hayakawa, Carol Mosely Braun, Corky Gonzales, Thurgood Marshall, and the many others who successfully faced their challenges. When we are still, we can feel their strength echoing in our heartbeats and can open our minds to the signs they have left on the path.

My role models guide me to victory.

AT SOME POINT, WE ALL HAVE TO DEAL with someone who is rude, annoying, or obnoxious. That person might be a relative, neighbor, employee, supervisor, sales clerk, doctor, or teacher.

The most important thing to keep in mind when dealing with someone who is difficult is: It's not about us. People who mistreat others have unresolved issues that are their hang-ups. There's no need for us to try and fix them.

What we *can* do is establish a clear boundary of appropriate behavior. We don't have to tolerate someone who is crude, patronizing, or disrespectful. We don't have to be afraid of pushy people. Without sinking to their level, we can stand up for ourselves.

Remember, it's not our responsibility to control other people's behavior. Our responsibility is to take care of ourselves.

I do not accept offensive behavior. I calmly, rationally assert myself.

Unfinished Business *December 3*

UNFINISHED BUSINESS. LOOSE ENDS. Things left unsaid.

We are coming to the close of the year. Let's not let the year end without finishing what we have started. Sometimes it's difficult to follow through on projects. We procrastinate or "forget" them altogether. Today, let's commit to tying up loose ends. Let's fulfill our obligations to others and ourselves.

Let's also use today to resolve relationship issues. If we need to make amends, let's do so. If we need to tell somebody how we feel, let's do so. Let's clear out old messages and get rid of useless baggage. Let's put the past behind us and get ready to move into the future.

Talk about it. Write about it. Finish it.

I complete what I need to so that I can enjoy today and prepare for tomorrow.

IF YOU PUT A FROG IN A PAN OF BOILING water, the frog will jump out to save its life. But if you put a frog in a pan of cool water and slowly increase the temperature, its body will adjust to the heat, and it will stay in the water and boil to death.

Some of us are on a slow burn, passively adjusting to the hazards in our lives—pollution, violence, crime, addiction—waiting for somebody to tell us what to do, waiting for somebody else to take action, waiting for the problems to correct themselves. How hot does it have to get before we will react and save our planet, our neighborhoods, our children, ourselves?

If we feel overwhelmed or inadequate, we can remember Martin Luther King Jr. and César Chávez. We can think about the people in our communities who refuse to give up the fight for affordable housing, safe streets, or drug-free schools. One person *can* make a difference. *You* can make a difference.

The clock is ticking and the temperature is rising…what are you going to do about it? We must accept the reality that society's ills will not disappear unless we all accept responsibility.

I am of service to those in need.

筆

JOURNAL ENTRIES ARE NOTES TO OUR FUture selves. We can look back and commune with the person we used to be. We can look back and see how ideas have been percolating in our subconscious minds for weeks, months, or years.

We can learn from the insights we had during certain experiences that we may not remember now. When we are going through a hectic or traumatic time, we may become aware of a great many things, but if we don't write them down, we run the risk of missing the important lessons to be learned. Even entries we think are mundane—what happened at work today, what movie we watched last night—could shed light on our growth and development when we read them months or years later.

A journal is like an oyster: Open it and what looks like plain sand could become a pearl. Keep a journal. You might be surprised at the gems you find.

I write down my thoughts, dreams, and activities today. Tomorrow, I will be grateful.

Pamper Day *December 6*

THIS IS COLD AND FLU SEASON, BUT IF OUR immune systems are strong, we can go through winter without succumbing to the bugs that go around. Let's use this Pamper Day as a reminder to take care of ourselves.

Today, let's take inventory of our health habits. Are we eating properly? Getting appropriate levels of rest and exercise? If we've been allowing our careers, families, and the holidays to stress us out, let's take time out just for ourselves. Let's pick one healthful activity and do it today. Eat a cup of chicken soup. Incorporate a brisk walk into your trip to the mall. Buy yourself a present, wrap it, and put it under the tree. Take a short nap after work. Get a facial or massage over the lunch hour.

Give yourself permission to be well. A happy, relaxed person is a healthy person, which is the best present you can give to your loved ones and yourself!

Today I do something that makes me feel good.

Be Yourself — *December 7*

My perceptions of the world are my own and, consequently, I am not accepted by many Chicanos. It is not my responsibility to change to fit others' expectations of me; it is only my responsibility to be who I am, to respect others for who they are on their own terms, and to encourage the acceptance of all people who care to engage in self-discovery.

—JOHN DAVID MENDOZA BRODEUR

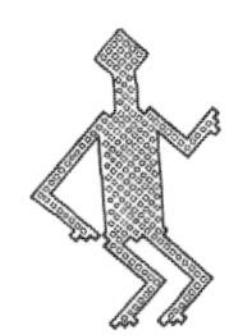

SOMETIMES OUR OWN PEOPLE MAY BE prejudiced against us because we don't measure up to their idea of what an African-American, Native American, Asian-American, or Latino *should* be. They may try to change us, saying we aren't "black/red/yellow/brown enough." This type of stereotypical thinking is just as senseless as when the dominant culture tries to fit us in boxes. We are individuals with the right to our own unique attitudes and opinions.

Nobody has the authority to grant us "official" ethnic status. We don't have to meet any externally imposed standards. Our only responsibility is to live up to our own expectations and be true to our own principles. Our only responsibility is to be ourselves.

I honor my unique personality and own my right to be who I am.

IT'S DIFFICULT TO WATCH PEOPLE WE love destroying themselves. Most of us are willing to do anything we can to help our friends and loved ones. However, sometimes in our efforts to help, we can hurt. Sometimes people need to suffer from the consequences of their actions so they can learn. If that is the case, the best thing we can do is let go.

When a friend is hurting, it is natural to want to fix their problems, ease their pain. But what we perceive as misery actually might be training. People may need to agonize for a while before they realize they need to change. They may never become willing to act if we keep cleaning up their messes for them.

Some people call letting go using "tough love." People in Twelve-Step programs call it detachment. We detach ourselves from people's problems so they can learn how to take care of themselves. If we need to detach from people today, we can do so knowing we are committing an act of love. Hard as it may be, we may have to let our friends fall a couple of times so they can become stronger and wiser.

I love people enough to be tough with them when it would help them.

GRACE IS A VIRTUE BESTOWED ON US by God—a power that can lift us up and move us toward our destiny in life. Grace might feel like an unexpected gift. We might think "why us?" But why not us? Grace is a gift we all deserve. We are children of God. We don't have to earn grace. We only have to be aware and be open to receive it. Grace operates within and around every living thing, today we can let it work its magic on us.

I exult in God's grace.

We Count *December 10*

Ain't I a woman? —SOJOURNER TRUTH

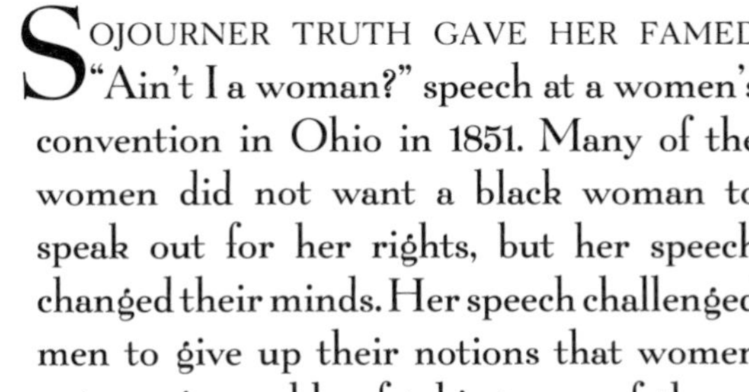

SOJOURNER TRUTH GAVE HER FAMED "Ain't I a woman?" speech at a women's convention in Ohio in 1851. Many of the women did not want a black woman to speak out for her rights, but her speech changed their minds. Her speech challenged men to give up their notions that women were frail creatures incapable of taking care of themselves. She challenged the white women in the audience to acknowledge that she was every bit as worthy to speak as they were. Sojourner Truth may as well have been asking "Don't I count?"

You bet, she counted! She went on to become a minister, an Abolitionist, and a feminist. She was born a slave but died a free woman—in every sense of the word.

We count, too. Let's not let anybody tell us differently. What we think, feel, hope for, and dream about matters. We are important.

I honor myself and require that others treat me respectfully.

THIS BOOK DOES NOT ADVOCATE abandoning discipline in the search for self. We don't have to quit our jobs, leave our families, and live in a spiritual commune to find ourselves. We must follow our hearts and listen to our inner selves, but we also must have discipline. Indeed, discipline is required for self-discovery.

Self-actualized people are disciplined people. Discipline doesn't mean monotony. We don't have to get up at the crack of dawn and live on oat bran. We don't have to be monks. We don't have to follow the regimen of soldiers. However, we benefit from methodically evaluating our actions. We benefit from reasoning our way through problems. It takes discipline to do the inner work required to know ourselves, to take responsibility for ourselves. It takes discipline to follow the journey of the heart.

Today, let's be disciplined, honest, and courageous. That's how we'll build our characters and determine our true purpose.

I welcome discipline as another tool for growth.

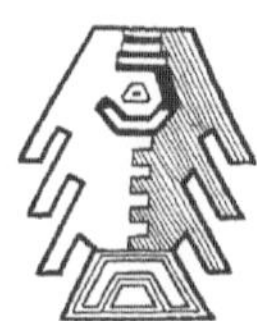

WE GET DOUBLE MESSAGES FROM people when they aren't being honest about their feelings with us or themselves. We get double messages when:

1. People's body language and words don't match. She says she's not mad, but her fists are clenched and her jaws are tight.
2. People act one way, but say something different. He says he likes you, but he never calls.
3. People say mean, rude things and call them jokes. But we don't feel like laughing.

Double messages are confusing and damaging to relationships. If we are angry with someone or don't want to see him/her again, we can tell them. We don't have to mask our feelings with politeness or so-called humor. We needn't make people guess our intentions.

I'm up front about my feelings and my meanings are clear.

Pride *December 13*

THE CHANT OF THE SIXTIES WAS "black is beautiful." Of course the same goes for brown, red, yellow, or white. We all can be proud of ourselves, our histories, and our cultures.

We display our feelings about ourselves through our body language and how we communicate. Are we slumped over, avoiding looking others in the eye? Do we stuff our feelings inside rather than speaking up for ourselves? We show pride by walking tall with our heads held high. We show pride by assertively and honestly saying what we need to say.

Take a few minutes to make an inventory of all the things you like about yourself. Write down all your positive qualities and keep this list near you at all times. If you begin to feel down about yourself, you can read a quick reminder of the characteristics for which you are proud. From that frame of reference you can make changes if you so choose.

I am proud of myself and show my pride in everything I do.

Onion Skin *December 14*

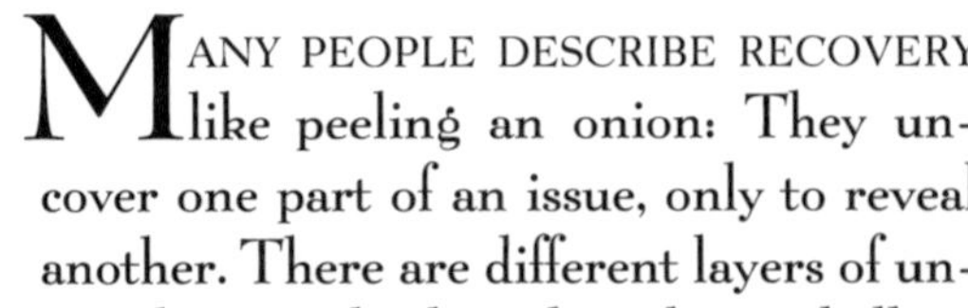

MANY PEOPLE DESCRIBE RECOVERY like peeling an onion: They uncover one part of an issue, only to reveal another. There are different layers of understanding. Just when we think we have learned all we need to know, we make a new revelation. Not even the wisest sage knows everything.

Some of us are afraid of what we will find when we expose the secrets and lies—afraid that we are rotten at the core. That is an old, false idea. We needn't be threatened by self-discovery. We will have to acknowledge our faults, errors, and limitations. However, we also will be able to own our knowledge, strength, and worthiness.

Today, let's peel off another layer and take another step toward wholeness.

I explore the deepest parts of myself, accepting myself completely.

Body Image *December 15*

TOO OFTEN WE CONNECT OUR FEELINGS about our bodies to how we feel about ourselves. Women are especially prone to thinking of themselves in terms of their appearance, but men also sometimes feel inadequate.

Women might feel insecure or ugly if they have big behinds, short hair, small breasts, skinny legs, or fat thighs. Men might believe they are unattractive if they are short, bald, have small penises, or pot bellies.

No matter what our bodies look like, we can still love ourselves. Our physical appearance has nothing to do with our worth or our likability. We are lovable and beautiful because we are children of God. It's time to end the self-abuse of hating our bodies. If we'd like to lose or gain a little weight, we can gently acknowledge that we want to change. We don't have to engage in torturous diatribes about how ugly we are.

Today, let's love all of ourselves: our imperfections as well as our virtues.

I love and appreciate my beautiful God-given body.

If we are workaholics or overachievers, we may feel unable to stop working. We may feel guilty if we aren't laboring and turn what could be a fun celebration into more work. Instead of enjoying the holidays, we may overdo and wind up feeling stressed and spent.

We can stop working so hard and play! We can give ourselves permission to have fun this time of year. We have the right to enjoy the spirit of the season. Happiness and excitement are all around us. We can share in the celebration. Today, let's party, laugh, and rejoice. Go to a movie. Light a fire in the fireplace and cuddle up with a loved one or a good book. If you think Christmas is just for children, act like a kid. Go see Santa. Have a treat.

Today or any day of the year we are entitled to cast our burdens aside, put down our load, and take a day off.

I celebrate the spirit of the season.

Signs *December 17*

IT IS SMART TO BE WATCHFUL OF THE signs in our path, but there's a difference between being superstitious and being spiritually aware.

Not every event foreshadows another. For example, a flat tire on the way to the wedding doesn't necessarily mean the universe is trying to warn us against marriage. But if we feel like we have giant birds flying around in our stomachs instead of butterflies, perhaps we should rethink our decision. Our uncomfortable *feeling* is the sign our inner selves are giving us.

Bad omens aren't what we need to be worried about. Our intuition and a realistic review of the facts will tell us how to act. We need to make decisions based on what feels right for us. If our guts are telling us something is wrong, we need to listen. We need to follow our instincts.

My intuition helps me make good decisions.

Because you can't hate the roots of a tree, and not hate the tree. You can't hate your origin and not end up hating yourself.

—MALCOLM X

ALEX HALEY'S BOOK *ROOTS* STARTED a trend among African-Americans to trace their lineage as far back as possible. People became familiar with great-great-grandparents who were slaves. They learned about their African ancestors' customs and practices. Other ethnic groups also researched their family histories to their origins.

Learning about our family trees is good for us. We may discover our relatives accomplished amazing feats of which we can be proud. We may learn the original purpose for family traditions and gain a better understanding of our kin and ourselves. Even if we discover some negative things about our family, we will grow from the experience.

Knowing our history helps us love and appreciate who we are. When we love our roots, we love ourselves.

I am the fruit of my family tree. I explore my roots with love.

Memories *December 19*

THE HOLIDAYS STIR UP LOTS OF memories. We may have happy recollections of "the good old days," when we were children opening presents on Christmas morning or sharing a meal with our families. We may fondly remember relatives who have since died or moved away. We also may have sad memories of being poor or neglected during a time when people are expected to give and receive presents. This time of year also can bring to the surface long-repressed childhood disappointments.

We are blessed when we have pleasant memories; the affectionate, contented feelings they generate in us can warm us during these winter months and cheer us anytime we feel blue. If, however, we tend to feel melancholy this time of year, we can use our unhappy memories to help us work through unresolved issues. We can choose to get through the pain by addressing the hurts, failures, or mistreatment we have experienced.

There is no reason for us to feel sad year after year. Let's do whatever we have to this year so that next year will be more enjoyable. Let's not let unpleasant ghosts haunt our holidays. It's time to put them to rest...for good.

This is a good day to explore my memories and determine what I have yet to work through.

THERE IS A PROCESS TO MAKING DECIsions. First, we collect information, starting with ourselves. How do we feel? What do we think? Is our intuition telling us anything? We also can ask trusted advisors what benefits or drawbacks they see. We can go to the library and research data that might influence our decision.

Then, we weigh the facts. One way to do this is to make a list of the pros and cons so we can see hard evidence of the results of the decision. If we have an equal number of pros and cons, we can factor in our "gut feelings" to help us choose.

Next, we stay flexible about our decisions. We may choose something and discover it doesn't feel right. We may change careers and find out we don't enjoy our new field. We may regret leaving a marriage or moving to another city. Trial and error is how we learn. If we make a decision and it turns out to be unsuccessful, we have the power to evaluate and make *another* decision to change our predicament.

Finally, we find a balance between giving ourselves enough time to make a wise choice and procrastinating. Waiting until the time is right is intelligent; stalling the decision because we are afraid is ineffectual.

I make decisions with care and confidence.

Forgiveness *December 21*

WE WILL BE HURT. THAT'S TO BE EXpected. People are human and they will do things that offend us. If we meditate on the Serenity Prayer, we will know that we cannot control others, but we can control ourselves. If there is healing that needs to happen in a relationship, we can do our part by forgiving.

Many of us don't want to forgive. Holding on to our grudges gives us a sense of power over people. We may feel that if we forgive what others did to us, we'll be letting them off the hook. The truth is that when we forgive others, we let ourselves off the hook. When we hold on to resentment, we create a psychological bond to the person we claim to despise. It keeps us locked into the game.

If a parent, spouse, friend, or lover did us wrong, we can tell them what they did, why it hurt, and then let go. If they aren't willing to make amends or what they did was so grievous that we no longer want to be with them, we can end the relationship. We don't have to like, respect, or trust them again. But in order for us to truly put it behind us, we must forgive them.

With my own self-interest at heart, I forgive those who trespass against me.

SOMETIMES WE MAKE THINGS MORE complicated for ourselves than they need to be. We try to do too much at once. Today, let's give ourselves permission to focus on this day only. If what we need to accomplish today still feels like too much, we can focus on one hour at a time. We can more easily achieve our goals when we concentrate on one at a time.

Concentrating on one goal, one activity at a time, simplifies life. Keeping life simple is a goal of recovery, and a major tenet of Eastern and Native American philosophies.

When we keep it simple, our lives are easier to manage because we don't overwhelm ourselves with countless activities. When we keep it simple, we minimize the number of things that can go wrong and therefore lessen our worries. When we keep it simple, we enable upbeat attitudes and lighthearted thinking. When we keep it simple, we are more calm, effective, and in charge.

Life is complicated enough; let's not add to the confusion.

I simplify my life by concentrating on one thing at a time.

Anger at Family Members *December 23*

ALMOST ALL OF US CARRY SOME SCARS from childhood. Some are small grievances where we were disappointed or hurt. Some parental errors—physical, verbal, or sexual abuse, and neglect—are despicable, and it may take ages to heal those wounds. In the course of therapeutic exploration, we typically discover that we hold some anger toward our parents or other family members.

We explore our angry feelings not to get revenge on our parents, but to mend our wounds. Our healing depends on facing angry feelings. Exploring anger left over from childhood is a painful process, especially if abuse was involved. It will help to work through it with someone we trust.

It hurts to look back at our childhoods and acknowledge that we were mistreated, ignored, tormented, or deceived. Under such circumstances, it's natural and understandable to be angry.

Today, we can explore our anger at family members. We can release our anger and heal. Write about it in a journal. Tell your Higher Power. Tell a therapist or support group friend.

I explore and express my anger toward my parents or other family members and enjoy the healing power of the truth.

Envy — *December 24*

A well-nigh universal human stupidity is the belief that our neighbor's success is the cause of our failure.

—CHARLES V. ROMAN

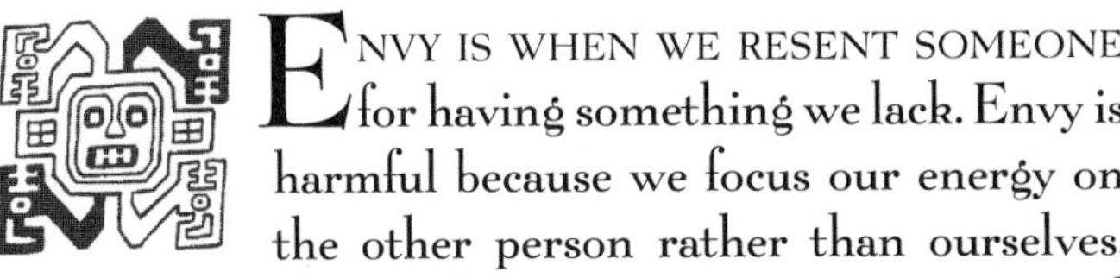

ENVY IS WHEN WE RESENT SOMEONE for having something we lack. Envy is harmful because we focus our energy on the other person rather than ourselves. We become victims and martyrs, giving up our potential to achieve.

So what if someone has more or better than we do? What effect does that have on us? Believing that other people's good fortunes take something away from us is based on an illusion of scarcity and lack. There is room in this world for all of us to be successful, happy, peaceful, and prosperous.

However, our spiteful feelings are a good determinant of what is missing in our lives. Material goods, talents, skills, jobs, relationships—whatever other people have that we want—we can have, too. In order for us to acquire them, we must stop begrudging others happiness. We can't reach our goals by holding on to negative emotions.

I celebrate the accomplishments of others and focus on achieving my goals.

Christmas *December 25*

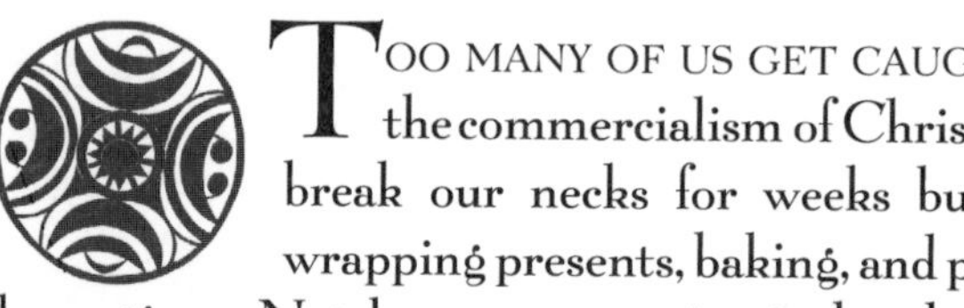

TOO MANY OF US GET CAUGHT UP IN the commercialism of Christmas. We break our necks for weeks buying and wrapping presents, baking, and putting up decorations. Not because we enjoy it, but because we think we have to. In our fervor to have the "perfect" holiday, we miss out on the true meaning of the season.

On the other hand, people are more charitable, gracious, and loving this time of year. The spirit of Christmas is giving. And not just giving the best, most expensive gifts. But giving our time, attention, care, and love to people. We know this, but we don't always behave like it. Let's make this the year we actually act on this philosophy. Today, let's give love.

Let's celebrate the generosity and caring of this holiday, today and every day.

I make this a truly Merry Christmas by committing myself to love today and the rest of my life.

TODAY IS THE FIRST DAY OF KWANZA, AN African-American celebration of traditional African values that is commemorated by people all over the world. The seven-day holiday, which runs through January 1, is based on the *Nguzo Saba,* the "seven principles." The seven principles, each celebrated on a different day, are: *Umoja* (unity), *Kujichagulia* (self-determination), *Ujima* (collective work and responsibility), *Ujamaa* (cooperative economics), *Nia* (purpose), *Kuumba* (creativity), and *Imani* (faith).

We don't have to be African-American to celebrate these values, we all can benefit from reflecting on these principles. Today, let's take inventory of the principles that are guiding our lives. Let's question our beliefs and values.

What is your philosophy of life? What has meaning and merit to you? How do you want to live your life? During Kwanza, let's try to answer these important questions.

For the next week, I reflect on unity, self-determination, responsibility, cooperation, purpose, creativity, and faith.

Mindfulness *December 27*

MINDFULNESS IS BEING SINGULARLY aware of the activity we are involved in. Mindfulness is being completely present in the moment.

With mindfulness comes more effective work and more satisfying relationships. Things flourish when we pay attention to them. The teacher who all the students love, the woman with the green thumb, and the basketball player who scores fifty points a game practice mindfulness. We can too.

Today, let's be in the moment. Let's choose one activity and devote ourselves to it completely. If we are eating an apple, let's feel and hear the crispness when we bite it. Taste and smell its sweet, juicy flesh. If we are watching a movie, let's tune out all other distractions and concentrate on the plot and characterization. If we are driving to work, let's pay attention to the traffic. Listen to the noise of the sirens and trucks. Look at the expressions of the other drivers. Notice the names of all the streets we cross.

Be mindful of what you do today.

I pay attention to my life.

Baby with the Bathwater *December 28*

MANY OF US ARE ON A QUEST FOR change. We want different or better or more for ourselves. This book encourages people to seek fresh ideas and new ways of being, however, let's be careful that in our search for the new, we don't get rid of all of the old.

Let's not throw out the baby with the bathwater.

We have issues yet to work through, skills yet to practice. But we also have many positive, healthy characteristics—humor, honesty, diligence, caring—that sometimes get overshadowed by the traits we want to change. We can focus on self-improvement and still stay aware of our beneficial behavior patterns. We can foster a realistic image of ourselves that includes our positive and negative traits.

To help us maintain reasonable goals for ourselves, we can remember the saying: "I may not be perfect, but parts of me are excellent."

My goal is to refine myself, not reject myself.

Shoulds December 29

PEOPLE IN TWELVE-STEP GROUPS SAY "Don't should on Me" as an entreaty for others to respect their boundaries. (It's a takeoff of the Revolutionary War saying "Don't Tread on Me.") Twelve-steppers know they have the right to determine things for themselves.

People who were reared in dysfunctional families get "shoulded on" all the time because there aren't healthy limits between people. Parents must give guidance and direction to their children, but also allow them to think for themselves. Children can't learn how to do for themselves when parents are always telling them what to do.

We "should on" ourselves too, which creates an expectation for ourselves. Here are some phrases that might work better than "I should": "It would be healthier for me to…" "I would benefit more from doing…" "I want to…" "It is in my best interest to…" "It's appropriate to…"

Let go of "should" today. We can allow our children to reason their way through problems. If friends come to us for advice, we can offer suggestions that might work for them, but only they can decide what is right for them.

I don't "should on" myself or others. I allow us all to do our best.

Aging *December 30*

Age ain't nothing but a number.

—AFRICAN-AMERICAN SAYING

THE END OF ANOTHER YEAR MAY bring to mind that we are getting older.... How wonderful!

How wonderful that we have the opportunity to experience the maturity and wisdom that comes with advanced age. Just think of all that we know now that we didn't know last year or the year before. We'll know even more next year.

It's unfortunate that American society's love affair with youth makes some of us fear getting old. After all, older folks have much to offer that smooth skin and firm bodies can't compete with. Besides, just because we are getting older doesn't mean we have to act "old." We can be feisty, sexy, vital, alive, zestful people well into our golden years. Look at Lena Horne, Tina Turner, Julio Iglesias, and other middle-aged performers who are at the height of their popularity.

We needn't be afraid to get old. As long as we make the most of each moment, we won't regret the ones that are behind us and we will look forward to those still ahead.

I thank God for allowing me to grow older. Every day is a celebration of my life.

THE LAST DAY OF THE YEAR. SO MUCH has happened for which we can be grateful and for which we can be proud.

As is customary, we might have started developing our New Year's resolutions. We're going to finally lose those ten pounds, quit smoking, start exercising.

Before we look to the future, let's use today to take stock of the year that has passed. What have we accomplished that makes us proud? What has our family done that makes us proud? As we close the year, let's be grateful for all it has given us.

As we say good-bye to another year, let's express our gratitude for the joys and lessons it brought.

I celebrate the happiness of the year that is ending and look with hope to the year that is beginning.

Topic Index

Glossary of Symbols

 *Eat*

 *Light*

 *Pen*

 *Water*

 *Taoist good luck charm which claims to cure all diseases. The joined circles symbolize stars. It reads "with the aid of the Heavenly Trinity, Shan Tseng, Yu Tsing and Tai Tsing, to chase out the demons, and to revive the dying."*

Permissions

Quote(s) by

Alvarez, Jr., Lt. Commander Everett; Vicki Carr; Jose Feliciano; Judge Harold R. Medina. From *Rising Voices* by Al Martinez. Used by permission of the author.

Angelou, Maya. Writer. Used by permission.

Baldwin, James. From *The Fire Next Time.* Used by permission.

Barstow, Rose Mary; Mary Morez; Dr. Constance Pinkerman; Tsewaa. From *I am the Fire of Time: The Voices of Native American Women,* edited by Jane Katz, Copyright 1977. Used by permission of the editor.

Big Elk, Chief Dan George, Chief Joseph, Chief Luther Standing Bear, Ohiyesa (Charles Alexander Eastman), Chief Seattle, Teedtuscung, Thayendanegea (Joseph Brant), White Shield, Winnebago Lesson. From *Native American Wisdom* by Kent Nerburn and Louise Mengelkoch, Copyright 1991. Reprinted by permission of New World Library, San Rafael, CA.

Boggess, Robert. Used by permission.

Brodeur, John David Mendoza. Used by permission.

Buddha. Used by Permission of Donald H. Bishop, Professor Emeritus, Philosophy Department, Washington State University.

Chavez, César; The Dalai Lama; Thich Nhat Hanh; Diane Nash. From *In the Footsteps of Gandhi* by Catherine Ingram, Copyright 1990. Reprinted by permission of Parallax Press, Berkeley, CA.

Cervantes, Lorna Dee. Excerpted from the poem entitled "Poem for the Young White Man Who Asked How I, an Intelligent, Well-Read Person Could Believe in the War Between the Races" from *Emplumada* by Lorna Dee Cervantes, Copyright 1981. Reprinted by permission of the University of Pittsburgh Press.

Crashing Thunder. Reprinted from *Crashing Thunder: The Autobiography of an American Indian,* edited by Paul Radin. Copyright 1926 by D. Aopleton & Co., renewed 1954 by Paul Radin. Used by Permission of the University of Nebraska Press.